Redhook

Redhook

Beer Pioneer

by Peter Krebs

Four Walls Eight Windows
New York/London

Published in the United States by
Four Walls Eight Windows
39 West 14th Street
New York, NY 10011
http://www.fourwallseightwindows.com

UK offices:
Four Walls Eight Windows/Turnaround
Unit 3 Olympia Trading Estate
Coburg Road, Wood Green
London N22 67Z

First printing November 1998.

Library of Congress Cataloging-in-Publication Data:
Krebs, Peter J., 1957-
Redhook : beer pioneer / Peter Krebs.
p.   cm.
Includes index.
ISBN: 1-56858-106-8
1. Redhook Ale Brewery—History. 2. Microbreweries—Washington (State)—Seattle. I. Title.
TP573.U6K74 1998
338.7'6633'09797772—dc21   98-36340
                                                          CIP

Printed in the United States
Text design by Acme Art, Inc.

10   9   8   7   6   5   4   3   2   1

To Gloria, who makes my life a magic carpet ride, and Michael, who steers the carpet.

Table of Contents

Preface

ON AUGUST 17, 1995, the Redhook Ale Brewery in Seattle, Washington, went public in one of the most widely anticipated stock offerings in Northwest history. On the first day of trading, Redhook's stock, which started with an Initial Public Offering (IPO) price of $17 a share, soared 50 percent to $27 a share. Within two weeks, Redhook's stock reached $35 a share. Many predicted that Redhook would be the next Starbucks, the highly successful Seattle-based coffee company that had gone public in 1992 and was conquering the world— one cup of coffee at a time. By comparison, Starbucks' stock, on its first day of trading, had risen from its IPO price of $17 a share to only $21.50 a share, and three months later—not two weeks—reached its first-year peak at $33 a share. Redhook, it was clear, was "red hot."

Typically after an IPO, the stock price shoots up and then slowly begins to drift down to a natural resting point, sometimes below the IPO price. Redhook stock, however, held its value, and after a few months, the price leveled off in the low thirties.

Which way the stock would go next—up or down—was anybody's guess. Redhook's share price depended on continued growth, and for Redhook to grow, it needed to leave the comfort of its own backyard and expand into national markets—just as Starbucks had so done following its IPO, when it went on a construction binge that resulted in chain of over 800 coffee shops across the United States by 1995.

There were many reasons to believe that Redhook would have the same success as Starbucks. Since 1987, the Redhook Ale Brewery, with its world-class line of ales, averaged an annual growth rate of about 40 percent, and within the past year, it had recently opened a new 250,000-barrel brewery in Woodinville, Washington, and it was building an identical brewery in Portsmouth, New Hampshire. Redhook also held a trump card over other craft breweries in the U. S. In 1994, Paul Shipman, Redhook's young, swashbuckling CEO, had entered into an exclusive distribution alliance with Anheuser-Busch, ensuring that Redhook products could reach the deepest recesses of the United States.

No one would dispute that Redhook had solid numbers, access to the best distribution network in the U. S., excellent production capacity, and top quality products, but Redhook's success wasn't in the numbers. It was in the beer, and for Redhook and its investors, the million dollar question was this: Would beer drinkers across the nation embrace Redhook with the same fervor as Northwest beer drinkers?

In the '80s and early '90s, a craft beer revolution swept through the Pacific Northwest. During the revolution, Redhook and other Northwest craft brewers converted legions of mainstream lager-swigging drinkers into ale aficionados with educated palettes. This new breed of brewers, led by Redhook, turned on a generation of Northwest beer drinkers to the wonders of full-bodied ale and freshness that resulted from a locally produced beer. In the process, they developed loyal customers and captured market share from imported beers such as Heineken and domestic lagers such as Budweiser.

Seattle, arguably, was the epicenter of the Northwest craft beer revolution. An exotic urban outpost of varied taste, cultural diversity, and eclecticism, Seattle was custom-made for a small, local brewery producing home-grown, high-quality ale. Its rainy, overcast weather, which drove people inside for months on end, didn't hurt the cause either.

In many ways, Redhook and the city of Seattle had come of age together. In the early '80s, Redhook was a struggling brewery in an old transmission shop in Ballard with a reputation for producing a beer that tasted like bananas and gave people headaches. Seattle, likewise, was a remote Northwest outpost on the way to Alaska, a blue-collar city predominately populated by Boeing workers. It was a city, some said, that lagged ten years behind New York and San

Francisco in terms of sophistication. It was a place, one East Coast writer had quipped, "where people went to hide or fail."

Much would change in a few short years. In the early '80s, personal computers were beginning to penetrate the market, and Microsoft, maker of MS-DOS (an operating system for the PC), experienced phenomenal growth on Seattle's east side. And Microsoft wasn't the only one; Attachmate, Wall Data, and WRQ, companies that created software enabling communication between PCs and mainframes, were also thriving. By the late '80s, Seattle had become a hotbed for software development and Seattle was on its way to becoming the next Silicon Valley—without the smog. At the same time, Boeing was posting record sales and hiring additional workers to meet the growing demand for its jumbo jets.

In addition to lucrative jobs in the software and aerospace industries, Seattle had other factors in its favor that attracted talented twenty- and thirty-somethings from around the country. In 1989, *Money* magazine voted Seattle the most livable city in the United States. It was a dubious, if not unwanted, distinction. For Seattle natives, it was like having a review of your favorite restaurant published in the paper. Suddenly Seattle became overcrowded with foreigners. By the late '80s, Seattle had become a mecca for New Yorkers and Californians seeking a better quality of life. The local sentiment to the influx of outsiders was best symbolized by graffiti on the bathroom wall at the University of Washington. "Happiness," it said, "is a New Yorker leaving Seattle with two Californians under his arms."

As one investment banker in New York City noted, Seattle had it all: Grunge music, Microsoft software, Starbucks coffee, and Redhook beer. Seattle, it seemed, had become a poster child for the postsmokestack industrial city, and its beverages of choice—Starbucks and Redhook—symbolized an affluent and sophisticated lifestyle. Traditional jobs in the fishing and logging industry were replaced by high-tech jobs in the software industry. And these high-tech jobs paid handsomely, creating a significant layer of young, well-educated workers with disposable income to spend on luxury items such a craft beer. These "techies" were a breed apart, with different purchasing habits than earlier generations of Seattleites. A typical software wonk drove a new, imported sports car, drank Starbucks coffee, and didn't flinch at the prospect of coughing up two bucks for a fresh, locally produced microbrew such as Redhook.

Perhaps young, affluent Seattleites with educated palettes were willing to pony up $7.99 for a six pack of Redhook, but how would Redhook fare with Joe Six Pack, or more accurately, Joe Chablis, across the country? After all, you could buy a six pack of Budweiser for half the price of Redhook. And didn't all beers taste pretty much the same?

At a dinner party at my home in Seattle in the summer of 1995, I debated with friends this issue of Redhook's price and their expansion into a national market. I took the position that Redhook's stock surge was a short-term phenomenon and that its expansion into national markets would be slow and difficult. Beer drinkers across the country, I argued, wouldn't pay $7.99 for a six pack of beer, especially a beer they'd never heard of. The rest of the country, I concluded, was not like Seattle. But the same argument had been used against Starbucks, my wife Gloria countered. Many claimed people outside of Seattle would never pay more than $2 for a cup of coffee. "Look how well Starbucks was doing," she said.

As I pondered a reply to Gloria's comment, our friend Paul Bulson interjected with a statement of sheer wonder. "Who would have ever thought," Bulson mused, "that Redhook would be where it is today?" Bulson, who had managed the Mark Tobey pub, a popular, upscale watering hole in Seattle's Pioneer Square in the '80s, recalled how Redhook's CEO, Paul Shipman, was a frequent visitor to the pub during Redhook's early days. "Shipman was always trying to get me to invest in the company," Bulson said, "but I wouldn't do it." Redhook Ale, Bulson remembered, was awful, almost undrinkable in those day, and investing in Redhook at the time hardly seemed like a wise idea. Bulson went on to explain that Shipman had started Redhook with Gordon Bowker, the same guy who started Starbucks. Bowker was the idea man, he explained, and Shipman was the master salesman who successfully convinced Seattleites to drink their weird tasting ale.

Days after the dinner party, the combination of Bowker and Shipman continued to intrigue me. How had they done it, I wondered? How had they successfully changed the drinking habits of an entire generation of Seattleites? How had they taken a little brewery in the early '80s that produced a weird tasting beer and parlayed it into one of the crown jewels of the Pacific Northwest? And what magic formula did Bowker possess that enabled him to start two wildly successfully beverage companies—one that made coffee, another that made beer?

The more I thought about it, the more it seemed that these questions might be the basis for a book, so I pieced together a quick proposal. Several weeks later, I met with Pam Hinckley, Redhook's marketing manager at Redhook's Trolleyman Pub in Fremont. Hinckely, a young, vibrant woman, was receptive to the idea of a book. She provided me with some starting tips for the first chapter, and then walked me through the Fremont Brewery on the way to Redhook's corporate offices—located across the parking lot from the brewery. Shipman was out of the office at the time, so Hinckley promised that she would pass the proposal along to him.

About three weeks later, I was sitting at home working on a computer book I was writing for Microsoft Press, when the phone rang. When I said "hello," a distinctive, booming voice came over the phone. It was Shipman. He was excited about the idea, and he was faxing the proposal immediately to Gordon Bowker. Shipman and I agreed to meet several weeks later to talk about our next steps for the book.

I first met Shipman in late June of 1996 at Redhook's Fremont offices. Shipman came out and greeted me, dressed in khakis and a button-down cotton shirt. In appearance, he reminded me of a young Orson Welles. Shipman and I talked in a Redhook conference room. We discussed the details of the book, and then I told him I had prepared fifty questions for our first interview. As it turned out, it took only one question to get him started.

"How did you get started in the beer business?" I asked, and Shipman launched into a one-and-a-half-hour monologue of the entire Redhook saga. It was obvious that he loved every minute of the story. It was a story about how two guys, himself and Bowker, who knew nothing about making beer, converted an old transmission shop into a brewery, bumbled their way through the first couple years, and went on to become one of the top-selling craft breweries in the United States.

At the time of our first interview, Shipman was on top of the world. Redhook's stock hovered in the high twenties and its shareholders were giddy with the stock's success. Redhook beer was being distributed, thanks to the Anheuser-Busch alliance, in forty-four states, and Redhook was experiencing a record-breaking quarter for sales, with a (soon to be announced) 54 percent increase in total sales and a 61 percent increase in net income over the 1995 second quarter results.

Over the course of the next year and a half, I conducted a number of interviews with Shipman, Bowker, and other key players at Redhook and learned the inside story about Redhook's early struggles, and its ensuing boom years. This book was originally structured as a modern-day success story. After all, Redhook blazed an innovative trail on its way to success. It was, for example, the first craft brewery to go public. In addition, no other craft brewer had built lavish, new breweries like Redhook had in Woodinville, Washington, and in Portsmouth, New Hampshire. And no other craft brewer had forged a creative, if not controversial, distribution alliance with Anheuser-Busch to distribute its brews across the nation.

When I first started interviewing Shipman and Bowker in the summer of 1996, Redhook was the envy of the craft beer industry. It owned three state-of-the-art breweries, it had a profile of eight styles of world-class beers, and its sales were going through the roof. But in the fall of 1996, Redhook's fortunes quickly changed. In September, a tidal wave of craft beer hit the market. Much of it came from hundreds of new brewers who witnessed the craft brewing craze in the early '90s and jumped into the fray to cash in on the bonanza. Ironically, as this tidal wave of beer rolled across America, consumers were losing interest in craft beers. Almost overnight, growth in the craft beer market went flat.

For Redhook and the craft beer industry, the results were disastrous. Following its record-breaking quarter in 1996, Redhook experienced declining sales. It lost money for three successive quarters. Sales of barrels of beer dropped in the range of 2,000 to 2,500 barrels a quarter. Shareholders abandoned the stock, causing the share price to tumble more than twenty points to as low as $6 a share. The craft beer industry, it was clear, had entered a shakeout phase, and many began to wonder not when Redhook's stock would rebound, but if the company would survive at all.

CHAPTER ONE

REDHOOK ALE BREWERY TRAIL

IT WAS A TRAIL OF PRIDE AND PASSION. A trail littered with success and failure. The trail stretched from a humble building in Ballard, Washington, that once served as a transmission shop; to a converted trolley barn a mile east in Fremont, Washington; to a stunning chateaulike brewery in Woodinville, Washington, about twenty miles northeast of Seattle; and finally across the country to a Woodinville Brewery look-alike in Portsmouth, New Hampshire.

No other craft brewery had boldly forged ahead quite like Redhook had, building new breweries that were not just high-tech wonders, but architectural statements in their own right. There were other craft breweries such as Boston Beer Company, makers of Samuel Adams brand, that produced more beer than Redhook. (Boston Beer Company in 1997 brewed 1,3552,000 barrels in comparison to Redhook's 214,600.) But no other brewery had taken the daring steps Redhook had, building not one, but two lavish, technically advanced breweries in different parts of the country—in addition to an existing brewery in Seattle, Washington.

For Paul Shipman, Redhook's CEO, building breweries was not only a way to keep up with the surging demand for Redhook's products, but also a way of carefully controlling, if not improving Redhook's quality. His approach to brewing beer was drastically different from that of Jim Koch, owner of the Boston Beer Company and a fierce Redhook competitor, and Shipman and Koch often sniped at each other in the press about their different methods of brewing beer. Koch, president and founder of Boston Beer, contracted out its production to other brewers' facilities, so he could concentrate on sales and marketing, rather than production. As a result, if demand dropped, he simply scaled back in one of the various breweries with whom he contracted to brew his beer.

But Shipman wasn't willing to give up control over the quality of his beer to another brewery as Koch had. Shipman wanted to control every aspect of the process, from the equipment used, the processes employed, to the people who brewed the beer. Shipman once compared brewing a beer such as Redhook ESB to the making of a house specialty in a fine restaurant: each time, every aspect of the preparation had to be near perfect. It wasn't enough to have fresh ingredients and follow the recipe. The equipment used had to be top quality to ensure precision, and the staff had to be carefully trained in order to execute the same dish flawlessly time and time again. Only by building their own breweries and training their own staff, Shipman believed, could Redhook achieve the level of quality he was after.

It was an expensive and risky strategy that resulted in high-quality beers, magnificent breweries, and a well-trained brewing workforce, but also a strategy that had dire consequences. As competition in the craft beer market increased in the late '90s, and demand for craft beer waned, Redhook was left with too many breweries and not enough demand. By March of 1998, Redhook was forced to close its Fremont Brewery, and its Portsmouth Brewery operated at only approximately 20 percent of its 250,000 barrel capacity.

Archeologists know that much can be learned from a civilization by the buildings it leaves behind. Shipman himself once told me that after twenty years, the only things that would matter in regard to Redhook would be the taste of the beer and the buildings left behind. With this idea in mind, I spent several days, through the course of my research, acting as an archeologist of sorts, and revisited Redhook's past by examining its buildings (all except its Portsmouth facility.)

In the summer of 1998, I visited Redhook's Woodinville Brewery, built in 1994, to see, firsthand, what Shipman was talking about when he raved about its architecture. Woodinville is a suburb about thirty miles northeast of Seattle, and Redhook's Woodinville Brewery was located just a few miles outside of downtown Woodinville in a pastoral area that is often called Napa North. Two wineries, in addition to the brewery, are clumped together just off Highway 202. The Columbia Winery to the west, is within eyesight of the Woodinville Brewery, and the Chateau Ste. Michelle Winery, to the southwest, is located just across the road from the Columbia Winery.

As you drive the winding road onto the impeccably kept grounds of the Redhook Woodinville Brewery, you see a massive white stucco building with steep-pitched, triangular roofs of green corrugated metal. Modeled after the German Andechs Brewery, arguably the most beautiful brewery in all of Bavaria, the brewery looks like a modern-day wine chateau.

By craft brewing standards the brewery is gigantic—70,000 feet, with a capacity to brew 250,000 barrels of beer a year. Inside the brewery, I was met by David Mickelson, Redhook's chief operating officer, who gave me permission to wander the brewery unescorted. First, I wandered upstairs to the brains of the brewery—the brewhouse—where I found, in addition to that wonderful aroma of a brewery, a number of one-hundred barrel, partially submerged, stainless steel brewery vessels, huddled around a brewing console of three personal computers.

Head brewer, Dano Laxdall, sat in front of the computer monitors, two of which supplied feedback about the progress of the beer and the status of the equipment in the brewery. The center monitor showed a digital representation of the brewery, and Laxdall demonstrated with the track ball (a mouselike device for moving a computer cursor) how he could move the cursor on the screen to any area and click, to zoom in on any area of the brewery for more detailed status. To brew a new batch of beer, Laxdall explained, he used the computer to pick a recipe. Only one brewer at a time was required to run the automated system, capable of brewing ten one-hundred barrel batches of beer a day. I was witnessing, I decided, the new age of brewing. The brewing process could be done, almost entirely, by one man, sitting in front of a computer, with the click of the track ball.

Next I wandered down to the end of a long hallway to an observation deck, which looked over the bottling room, an area the size of a football field that hummed with automation. It looked like a complex city railway system, with the bottles and beer cases serving as train cars. Countless bottles lined up for filling, where they were picked up and filled by a giant rotating metal cylinder, and then sent down the line for the next step in the process. Automated stations along each area of track performed a specific function, with giant mechanical arms, for example, lifting two cases of beer bottles or more at a time and placing them into cardboard boxes. Finally, at the back end of the bottling room, cases of beer hurried up the conveyer belt to an area where they were stacked, and then eventually shipped by truck to customers.

Next, I took the elevator downstairs and explored the fermenting cellar, a room filled with two-story stainless steel fermentation tanks as far as the eye can see. The complexity and symmetry of the piping connecting the tanks was both staggering and beautiful, and I wondered how and who ever figured this all out.

When I had arrived at the brewery and told Mickelson I wanted to explore the premises, he instructed me, if I was stopped by workers, to tell them that I was writing a book, so it was okay for me to wander around. If there was a problem, he said, I should have the workers call him. The funny thing was, I hardly saw any workers in the brewery. I saw one guy—total—in the bottling area. There was another, Dano Laxdall, in the brewhouse. And I ran into a worker in the fermenting cellar. That was it, three production workers in a 70,000-square-foot brewery. At first, I figured that the workers must be on their lunch breaks, since I was visiting the brewery between twelve and one o'clock. But as I was leaving, I ran into a tour guide, just beginning a tour, and asked her if the workers were on lunch break, or if what I had witnessed was the normal amount of staff in the brewery. What I had seen, she explained, was more or less the number of people who normally ran the brewery at any given time. Now I knew what Shipman meant when he said Redhook's breweries could break even at a very low percentage of capacity.

In early spring of 1998, I explored Redhook's recently closed brewery in Fremont, a funky Seattle neighborhood of shops, homes, and small businesses located a few miles northwest of downtown Seattle. From the outside, the Fremont Brewery seemed to be a proud testimony of achievement. The vintage red brick building, once a trolley barn for Seattle's Electric Railway, stretched the length of a block. REDHOOK ALE BREWERY was proudly painted in giant white letters across the upper west wall of the brewery. Ivy crept up the brewery walls. It was an inviting building, tastefully restored, and it reflected an aura, at least on the surface, of corporate prosperity.

From outside the brewery, I could hear the pounding of hammers. Construction workers were converting a portion of the once-venerable brewery into offices. The workers had left the side doors of the brewery open, so I sneaked inside, unnoticed.

The Redhook Fremont Brewery, with a capacity to brew 75,000 barrels a year, was essentially a smaller version of Woodinville. In Fremont, however, the maze of stainless steel German brewing equipment was idle. Imposing rows of cylindrical brewing vessels sat empty, and in the south section of the building, the once state-of-the-art Krones bottling line, an imposing conglomeration of panels, knobs, gauges, and pipes, collected dust.

Wandering to the north end of the brewery, I discovered the brewing console. With its banks of buttons and LED indicators, it looked like something borrowed from NASA's mission control. It was here in the Fremont Brewery—starting in 1988—I remembered, that Redhook first automated their brewing processes, dramatically improving the quality of their beer. Only eighteen months after opening in 1988, this brewery would reach its capacity, forcing Redhook to expand again and build the larger, and more advanced brewery in Woodinville in 1994.

To truly appreciate how far Redhook has come in a few short years, you have to see the site of its original brewery. The same day I visited the Fremont Brewery, I stepped back further in time and explored the site of Redhook's original brewery in Ballard, a predominately Scandinavian neighborhood of small business, warehouses, shipyards, and to the north, homes. The original brewery was located in a converted transmission shop at the corner of 47th and Leary, about a mile to the west of the Fremont Brewery.

In the north section of the building I found Tad Dean's Ballard Way Body Shop, surrounded to the east and west by old cars, campers, snowmobiles, and every other imaginable form of scrap metal. Tad Dean, as it turns out, was a neighbor of Shipman's fifteen years ago when Shipman lived in Ballard, so he was more than willing to let me wander through the jumbled assortment of primed car chassis, car doors, compressors, old tires, and trash cans in his shop.

As I ambled through the building, my mind was filled with visions of the past—visions of makeshift equipment that was cobbled together to form the first brewery. I envisioned Charlie McElevey, Redhook's first brewmaster, adjusting the dials on Redhook's first brewhouse, a twenty-five-barrel copper unit, shaped like a bullet, that was built in Germany in 1950. I envisioned McElevey's assistants lowering hops into a homemade brew kettle, using makeshift cages of stainless steel. And I imagined Redhook's first batches of weird-tasting beer, sitting inside the wine tanks that had been modified for fermenting beer. And I imagined McElevey's assistants filling used, banged up kegs of beer by hand, and then hoisting them, again by hand, into a tiny cooler.

As I walked to the south section of the shop, followed by Tad Dean, I noticed a yellowish semicircle etched in the cement floor.

"That's where the old Redhook brewhouse used to be," Dean said proudly. As I continued wandering through the shop, reliving Redhook's past, I was reminded of something Shipman once told me during one of our interviews.

"There's no question," Shipman said, "when I look back at the old transmission shop, that it was a charming period. Sometimes when I've had a bad day dealing with the hassles of the board, or I'm having problems with investors, I think about going back to the old days. Entrepreneurs often talk about the romance of the early garage phase of their business when it was struggling to survive. But the truth of the matter is that when the entrepreneur is in the garage phase, his motivation to succeed is incredibly powerful. Because the garage phase is so painful, all you want to do is get out of it—as fast as you can. The truth of the matter is, it's hell."

CHAPTER TWO

THE CURSE OF THE ENTREPRENEUR

FROM EARLY CHILDHOOD, Paul Shipman was pushed to succeed. He was a baby boomer, born in 1953, who was raised with the belief that he was part of a powerful legacy of successful professionals. His father was a corporate lawyer for United Engineers, a large Philadelphia consulting company. His mother was a college English professor at Cheney State University. His parents had tabulated the history of family success back through the generations and held it up as an example of what the family stood for. As a paragon of success, they often invoked the name of Shipman's great, great uncle Mario Peruzzi, who at one time had served as the president of Planter's Peanuts. "You can do anything you want," his parents would exhort, "you have the greatness of Uncle Mario in your genes."

As a child, he had shown tremendous promise. Even before beginning kindergarten, he could add large numbers in his head. On car trips, his parents occupied him by throwing out huge numbers for him to add or subtract, and he'd snap back the correct answer almost instantly, leaving others in the family to calculate the answer with pencil and paper to prove he was right—which he almost always was.

Even as a child, he was fascinated by numbers and business. His mother would later recall that as a young boy, he ran around the house yelling "I want XROX," the ticker tape symbol for Xerox. By the time he was in grade school, he was studying the stock market each day, pouring over the numbers on the stock page of the *Philadelphia Inquirer*. His parents had taught him what the various numbers meant and he studied the price earnings ratios of companies, looking for the hottest stock picks. By the time he was eleven, he got a paper route, and put his stock market acumen to work by investing in Sperry Rand, a stock he'd been following for years.

In addition to a keen understanding of numbers, Shipman had a silver tongue, and his powerful gift of persuasion made him a natural leader. In high school, he served as president of his junior and senior classes. Before the start of his junior year, Shipman and his friends, who called themselves "the associates," got together and divided up the power positions in the school. Shipman, of course, was at the helm as president, while one friend served as vice president, and another became editor of the student newspaper.

Although a math whiz, Shipman majored in English Literature at Bucknell University, and spent his junior year in Paris, studying at the Sorbonne. He took classes in French language, history, and civilization and learned about the world from the French perspective. He studied drawing and indulged his interest in cinema, arranging an apprenticeship in the editing department of Claude LeLouche's Film Treize studio.

Shipman's stay in Paris had a profound impact upon him. The early 1970s were a pivotal time in world history and he watched events unfold around the world on French TV. War had erupted in the Middle East between the Arabs and the Israelis; an oil embargo by the Arab oil-producing nations had precipitated an oil crisis in the United States; and Watergate was beginning to bubble up as a story of epic proportions.

Exposure to French culture, with its emphasis on food, wine, and leisure, forced Shipman to view his own culture differently. By the time he returned home in the summer of 1974, his perception of the United States had changed radically. He experienced reverse culture shock. The U.S., he concluded, had things backward. In France, everything was expensive, wages were low, and yet the people seemed to live well. The food, the wine, the pace, the culture—all supported a high quality of life. In the U.S., on the other hand, wages were high, prices were low, and yet people seemed to live so poorly. Everything in the States, he believed, was designed to be fast and inexpensive. The American passion for speed and efficiency had created tremendous wealth, but, in his opinion, it also demeaned the quality of life. During his stay in France, Shipman learned what quality of life meant, and he came to the conclusion that it was sadly lacking in the States.

Shipman developed an appreciation for wine in France, but at that time in his life, it hadn't occurred to him to pursue it as a career. His passion remained with beer. Before the start of his senior year at Bucknell, his parents prodded him about his career goals. He told them that after he graduated, he wanted to work in marketing for a brewery, so his parents arranged for him to meet Bob Taylor, a family friend and a distributor for Wagner Wine and Spirits. Taylor discouraged Shipman from a career in the brewing industry. It was stagnant, he told him, and it offered limited opportunities. The wine business, Taylor convinced Shipman, was where the action was. To jump-start Shipman's career, Taylor set up him up as a wine representative for Wagner Wine and Spirits on the Bucknell campus. At the time, campus beer representatives were commonplace, but campus wine reps were a rarity.

After graduation, Shipman continued his career in the wine business with Pequea Valley Vineyards in Lancaster, Pennsylvania. When owner Pete Wood, a Bucknell alumni, interviewed Shipman, he asked him how much money he wanted to make. Shipman told him he didn't care how much money he made, he loved the wine business and he wanted to work at Pequea. Wood put Shipman to work picking grapes, pruning vines, and working on the bottling line. He paid him, Shipman would later remember, next to nothing.

Shipman didn't make it past the summer. He was fired after a confrontation with his foreman about pruning techniques. Shipman learned his technique from a book. He insisted he was right and the foreman was wrong. Shipman interpreted his termination as a clear signal that he would never be happy unless he ran his own business. He also didn't particularly care that he was fired. Because in the fall, he was entering the MBA program at the University of Virginia.

Shipman's destiny was tied to the vine. In the middle of his first year of the MBA program, he met with his advisor, Stewart Shepard, to discuss his career goals. Shepard, the dean of the business school, was an amiable Welshman who was well connected in the business community. When Shipman told Shepard that that he'd been in the wine business and wanted to return to it when he graduated, Shepard lined Shipman up with a phone interview with Wally Opdycke, the CEO of Chateau Ste. Michelle Winery in Woodinville, Washington.

Opdycke hired Shipman over the phone. "I don't know what we'll have you do," Opdycke told him, "but why don't you come out for the summer and we'll get to know each other."

Shipman's father, who had often traveled to Washington State on business, had often regaled him with tales of the natural beauty of Seattle and the Pacific Northwest, so Shipman was eager to travel west for a summer adventure. Shipman also believed that the West Coast was better suited to his personality, talents, and ambitions than the East Coast. In his opinion, the West Coast offered a shortcut to success. In Philadelphia and other cities on the East Coast, Shipman believed, no one would take him seriously until he was forty years old. The wide open, unbridled, West Coast was more his style. On the West Coast, he thought, age was not a barrier to success.

As an easterner, Shipman had grown up believing that he was better than other Americans and he was determined that he was going to go out west and show them how things were done. Shepard, aware of the young man's impatience and take-charge attitude, felt compelled to offer Shipman a piece of fatherly advice before he headed west. He warned Shipman not to go out to Ste. Michelle looking to take over. That's what people on the West Coast expected from people on the East Coast, Shepard warned.

"Don't go out there looking like you want to take over, lad." Shepard warned. "That's what they expect from people from the east."

In June 1976, Shipman traveled cross-country in his Chevy pickup truck. When he reached eastern Washington, he thought he was in paradise. Driving the long, straight stretch of Interstate 90 through the rolling wheat fields, Shipman marveled at the natural beauty and inhaled the warm, clean air. But as Shipman crested Snoqualmie Pass, one of the portals through the Cascade Mountain range, he was greeted with typical western Washington weather. It poured.

Coming from a large city like Philadelphia, Shipman expected Seattle to be a Hooterville, a makeshift town in the middle of nowhere. Instead, he was surprised to see a city skyline with high-rise buildings shrouded in gray rain clouds. In the mid 1970s, Seattle was still a slumbering city with a small-town feel. Seattle, at the time, was a city recovering from the hangover caused by the draconian Boeing cutbacks of the late 1960s and early 1970s. During those years, Boeing, Seattle's primary employer, cut its workforce from over 100,000 to less than 38,000, prompting a mass exodus from the city.

Isolated in the northwest corner of the country, Seattle was a geographical anomaly to the rest of the country. East Coast people, it seemed, could never decide where it was located on the map. "Seattle?" one easterner asked a friend who had recently relocated to the rainy city, "is that near Mt. Rushmore?" Sometimes tourists visiting the Pike Place Market on Seattle's waterfront, it was reputed, would look across Puget Sound at nearby Bainbridge Island and ask a local Seattleite: "Is that Alaska over there?"

When Shipman arrived in Seattle, the city was still a well-kept secret to the rest of the country. Underneath their umbrellas and hooded raincoats, Seattleites were furtively smirking. Because they knew what would take the rest of the country more than ten years to discover: It really didn't rain that much in Seattle, and when the skies were clear, which was much more often than Seattleites cared to let on, their city was one of the most scenic in the world. Mt. Rainier, a snowcapped volcano of 14, 410 feet, loomed on the southeast horizon. To the west, the ridge of the Olympic Mountain range back-dropped Puget Sound and its nearby islands. The city was, without question, an undiscovered and unspoiled urban paradise. Hiking and skiing in the Cascade Mountains was only an hour's drive away. There was Puget Sound for boating enthusiasts and plenty of freshwater lakes for fishing and swimming. Houses were dirt cheap. Crime was virtually nonexistent, and traffic was never a problem. When hard pressed, some Seattleites would break down and let out the secret: Seattle was a damn nice place to live—that is, if you could withstand the long, dark, drizzling days of winter. And if you could find a job.

The following morning after arriving in Seattle, Shipman drove out to the Ste. Michelle winery in Woodinville. It was far grander than anything that he had imagined. The newly built French chateau with its twin turrets, stucco finish, and shuttered windows seemed almost like an illusion. In rural Woodinville, tucked away in the Pacific Northwest, stood a brand new eighteenth-century French chateau, looking as though it had been there for hundreds of years. At 152,000 square feet, it was one of the largest and most advanced wineries in the U.S.

To Shipman, Wally Opdycke, the CEO of Ste. Michelle, looked more like a summer intern than the head of a major winery. In his late thirties, Opdycke was a tall man with a Clint Eastwood build, dark eyebrows, and a terminally youthful face. His appearance, however, belied a razor-sharp financial acumen and the nerves of a riverboat gambler. Years later, many who worked with Opdycke during the early days of Ste. Michelle would look back and marvel at Opdycke's daring and savvy. "Ste. Michelle," many would later say, "was a tremendous gamble."

Having spent his career as an investment banker, Opdycke was well versed in how to research business opportunities and calculate risk, and he was convinced that his idea for a large scale winery in Washington State offered tremendous potential. He had every reason to trust his instincts. He had a proven track record of success and was well respected in the Seattle business community for his shrewdness and financial judgment. As the manager of the Fixed Income Portfolio for Safeco Insurance Company in Seattle, Opdycke had built his reputation, in part, by buying Boeing bonds in the late '60s when everybody else in the country was dumping them. Also in the '60s, he and his partner Kirby Cramer, also an investment banker at Safeco, had purchased Holly Research and Development, a small Seattle company that developed a cage that automatically fed and watered laboratory research rats. Through a series of leveraged buyouts, Cramer and Opdycke acquired research labs from TRW, Phillip Morris, and Ralston Purina, transforming tiny Holly Research into Hazelton Labs, the largest independent contract research facility in the world. In addition to building Hazelton Labs, Opdycke, along with a core group of people that included his partner Cramer and Seattle attorney Mike Garvey, had put together several other business deals, one of which involved the purchase of K2 skis on Vashon Island, Washington.

Opdycke quickly became Shipman's mentor. He took Shipman under his wing and energized in him the idea that he could do anything he set his mind to doing. As part of the internship, Opdycke let Shipman attend staff meetings and often shared his business philosophies with him. He also introduced Shipman to business colleagues and shared with Shipman his perspective of how these individuals fit into the overall Ste. Michelle picture. Shipman would always remember one comment Opdycke made to him about a particular individual. That guy is a really good guy, Opdycke had told Shipman, but he missed his chance to go for it. The comment caused Shipman considerable anxiety. Shipman worried that the world was going to pass him by. He vowed that by the time he was forty, he'd have an accomplishment under his belt on par with Opdycke's Ste. Michelle.

After studying the documents in Ste. Michelle's archives, Shipman, too, came to understand the magnitude of Opdycke's gamble. At the time that Opdycke started Ste. Michelle, the California wine industry was still in its infancy and there was no clear indication that boutique wines would be widely accepted in the U.S. In addition, many doubted that premium wine grapes could be grown successfully in Washington.

In the late '60s, Opdycke lived in San Francisco and spent time exploring California's Napa Valley. Trips to the Napa Valley kindled his interest in wine, and he discovered that the California wine industry offered tremendous financial opportunity. When Opdycke returned to Seattle, he began to wonder if a similar opportunity existed in Washington.

In 1970, Opdycke, who was then managing the Fixed Income Portfolio for Safeco Insurance in Seattle, wrote a letter to Dr. Walter Clore of the Irrigation Experiment Station in eastern Washington, asking about his grape-growing experiments and the types of grapes that he was growing. Opdycke didn't hear back from Clore until Clore unexpectedly showed up at Opdycke's office. Clore supplied Opdycke with information about the potential for investing in grapes and wine in Washington State. Research trips to eastern Washington further heightened Opdycke's excitement about growing premium wine grapes in Washington State.

Opdycke learned that the northern latitude of Washington State corresponds to the great wine-producing regions of Europe. Washington's Yakima Valley is on the forty-sixth parallel, while Bordeaux is at the forty-fifth, Burgundy at the forty-seventh, and the Rhine at the forty-eighth. That meant summer days, far longer than those in California, could produce grapes with plenty of sugar. Also, the cool nights of the Yakima Valley slowed the conversion of acid in the grapes to sugar, thus producing grapes high in sugar *and* acid—a classic combination. There were other advantages to the Yakima Valley: the land was much cheaper than in the Napa Valley; the soil was sandy, so roots could go down deep where they were not affected by fertilizer and surface water; the cool fall days for harvesting meant the grapes could arrive at the winery without fermenting en route, as happened in hot-harvest California; and irrigation, already heavily developed in the Yakima Valley, was much more reliable than rainfall.

Finally, the gradual rise and fall of heat in the spring and autumn was perfect for the delicate periods of blossoming and harvesting.

The downside of the opportunity was that bitterly cold winters gripped the Yakima Valley each year. Many Yakima Valley farmers maintained that the grapes would be wiped out by the first arctic express, a cold front that periodically sweeps down from Canada. But Clore convinced Opdycke that he had solved the freezing problem by, among other things, mounding the vines in dirt each winter and stressing the vines into early hardening each fall.

Encouraged by the research findings, Opdycke put together a group of Seattle investors and engineered a leveraged buyout of American Wine Growers, a struggling winery located in the industrial belt of Seattle. Its owners, a partnership of men in their seventies and eighties, had been unwilling to invest the time and money required to make the transition from fruit and dessert wines to premium wines. So they were happy to sell the company to Opdycke and his partners.

Opdycke named the new winery after American Wine Growers' fledgling label, Ste. Michelle, and became its CEO, working at the company part-time while he continued to work full-time at Safeco. To transform American Wine Growers into a world-class winery, Opdycke needed an infusion of cash. In 1973, after struggling for several years selling the winery's former brands of Pommerelle and Nowico wines, Opdycke wrote a new business plan for Ste. Michelle proposing that they finance its expansion by selling stock options. The stock offering was ill-timed. Opdycke ran into a soft stock market, brought on by excesses in the market and by the oil crisis that gripped the industrial world. Having failed to raise the necessary capital with a stock offering, Opdycke began to search for a wealthy corporate partner to finance his dreams for Ste. Michelle. Through a corporate agent, Opdycke and his partner attracted offers from Labatts, a Canadian brewing company, and U.S. Tobacco, a con-glomerate headquartered in Connecticut.

U.S. Tobacco made Opdycke an offer he couldn't refuse, so in 1974, he sold Ste. Michelle. Bankrolled by U.S. Tobacco, Opdycke significantly expanded Ste. Michelle's acreage and engaged in a program of heavy planting of delicate vinifera grapes—the European grapes required to produce premium table wines.

From the start, Ste. Michelle's white wines were extremely good, if not underrated. The turning point for the winery, however, came in 1974, when a bottle of 1972 Riesling won a first place competition in an important blind tasting held by the *Los Angeles Times*. The Ste. Michelle Riesling was not only the best tasting, it was also the least expensive. After the contest, Ste. Michelle wines became the darlings of wine experts around the U.S. and began to appear on the wine lists in the finest restaurants around the country. By the mid-1970s, the demand for Ste. Michelle wine outstripped the production capacity of the winery, and Ste. Michelle was forced to allocate its wine—an enviable position for a start-up winery.

During his internship in 1976, Shipman read every available document in the company archives. In the process, he became the company's unofficial archivist and historian. Shipman carefully studied the documents relating to the failed stock offering in 1973, as well as the materials associated with raising the capital to build the chateau in 1976. By studying the materials, Shipman felt he was able to understand Opdycke's vision for the winery at each point in its evolutionary process.

"By the end of the summer," Shipman would later say, "I think that more than anybody else at the company, I understood not only what Wally had accomplished, but also what he had tried to accomplish, but failed to do because of the oil crisis and the failed stock offering. While everybody at Ste. Michelle thought that attaining the resources of U.S. Tobacco was the most stunning of accomplishments, I understood what might have been—that Ste. Michelle could have been a public company—had it not been for the bad market period."

At the end of the summer, Shipman returned to the University of Virginia and completed his MBA, graduating summa cum laude. After graduation, Shipman returned to Ste. Michelle and took a full-time position as a marketing specialist, conducting research and identifying new business opportunities for the winery.

His first big career break came in 1979, when he was named brand manager for a line of jug wines that Ste. Michelle decided to develop. But before Ste. Michelle could develop the wines, they had to sell the idea to the parent company, U.S. Tobacco, so Shipman accompanied Opdycke to Connecticut, where he and Opdycke made the pitch for jug wines to a roomful of cigar-puffing tobacco executives.

Shipman explained to U.S. Tobacco that Ste. Michelle had the juice for the jug wine readily available—because to make really high-quality wines you always had some juice that didn't make the cut. Shipman also added that there was a significant number of cost-conscious consumers who drank wine daily. Shipman proposed that Ste. Michelle utilize this leftover juice to make an inexpensive, high-quality jug wine that would cater to daily wine consumers. Shipman proposed to address this market segment by packaging jug wine only in 1.5 liter bottles—larger than the standard 750 milliliter bottle of wine, but smaller than the 4 liter jug wines. There would be no advertising for this wine. It would take off, Ste. Michelle hoped, via word-of-mouth.

In the middle of the presentation, Shipman was interrupted by a U.S. Tobacco executive who wanted to know why U.S. Tobacco should invest another ten million dollars to make a jug wine when Ste. Michelle had been telling them all along that there was a growing market for premium wine.

"Counter segmentation," Shipman answered. "The strategy is counter segmentation."

The U.S. Tobacco executives each looked at one another, baffled, searching for someone who knew what counter segmentation was. Finally, they all turned to Barry Nova, the in-house marketing guru.

"Counter segmentation, is that like reverse interface?" Nova asked.

"No," Shipman shot back, "it's not like reverse interface." Counter segmentation, he explained, is what you do when the consumer was confused by having too many choices. You simplify the choices. And in the course of simplifying the choices, you lower the cost of the product. "We're only going to sell this product in big bottles," Shipman continued, "because in a big bottle you have as much wine as two little bottles, but you only have one cork, one label, and one bottle."

Then the U. S. Tobacco chairman, Lou Banal, asked Shipman and Opdycke to leave the room while they considered the proposal. After several hours of waiting, the upstarts from Ste. Michelle were called back in and told they had their money.

It was shaping up as a landmark year for Ste. Michelle. In addition to a secondary label, Ste. Michelle had decided to launch a national advertising campaign for its premium wines, at the behest of Barry Nova. To select an agency, they conducted an extensive interview process known as a bake-off. Opdycke invited the major Seattle advertising firms to participate. He also invited Heckler and Associates, a small agency started by two offbeat intellectuals, Gordon Bowker and Terry Heckler. Opdycke knew Heckler and Bowker from their advertising work at K2, the Vashon Island, Washington, ski manufacturer. Opdycke was a partner in a holding company that owned K2, one of Heckler and Associates' main accounts.

Seattle ad agencies bent over backward to win the prized Ste. Michelle account. Cole and Weber, the agency that eventually won the account, brought in a movies and a slide show. But Terry Heckler and Gordon Bowker of Heckler and Associates were of a completely different mold. While most Seattle agencies were doing their best to emulate their East Coast counterparts, Heckler and Associates were doing the complete opposite. They were a decidedly Northwest ad agency that was legendary in the Pacific Northwest for creating the wacky Rainier Beer commercials that had revived the ailing Rainier Brewery.

For their Ste. Michelle presentation, Heckler and Bowker walked in dressed in casual Northwest attire. Heckler carried a bottle of wine in a paper sack. Rather than presenting their concepts with a slide show or a movie, they just talked, and then unveiled the wine bottle in the sack, which featured a label they had developed called Paulouse Latrec, a tongue-in-cheek reference to the Palouse—a high plateau region in eastern Washington, and Toulouse Latrec, the French artist. Barry Nova and the Ste. Michelle executives were impressed by the presentation, and later decided to ask Heckler and Bowker to name and develop a label for their line of jug wines.

Bowker, the writing talent of the Heckler-Bowker team, was assigned as the contact point for the project. Shipman and his associates were excited to be working with Bowker, the eclectic and cerebral cofounder of Starbucks Coffee, then a small chain of retail stores in Seattle that sold gourmet coffee. Bowker had, after all, named Starbucks.

While Bowker dreamed up new names for the wine, Heckler worked on the artwork for the label. Shipman talked to distributors, studied the regional wine market, and crafted a marketing strategy. To help focus their thinking, Shipman came up with the theme for the new wine: It was a wine, he told Heckler and Bowker, for people whose taste had gotten ahead of their budgets.

For Bowker, the big decision was whether to retain the Ste. Michelle name for the jug wine label. Bowker believed that when a restaurant had Ste. Michelle on its wine list, brand recognition was high, but Ste. Michelle wanted the secondary label to exist as an independent entity to avoid any possibility of class contamination. Looking for a name that was free of immediate association, Bowker traveled to eastern Washington, where he discovered that the grapes for the wines were grown in Benton County about eighty miles southeast of Yakima in eastern Washington. And near the fields there were several ridges and a road named Farron Road. From these landmarks, Bowker concocted the name Farron Ridge.

In 1979, Ste. Michelle introduced a cork-finished bulk white wine name Farron Ridge into a crowded market, without advertising, and in the middle of a recession. By all rights, it should have fallen flat on its face. Instead, it flew off the shelves. According to Bill Stuht, Ste. Michelle's vice president of marketing, sales were fantastic—way beyond expectations. "It's been flying out of the winery," Stuht told reporters. "I guess it's just a case of being in the right place at the right time."

Bowker later told a reporter at the *Seattle Weekly* that the name Farron Ridge generated more interest than any product with which Heckler and Associates had worked. "Maybe it's because of the regional pride that it engenders," Bowker said. "I would write it off to natural inquisitiveness, but it's so disproportionate to anything I ever worked with. Maybe people think it's some place hidden down there they haven't discovered. Maybe in the future there will be a Farron Ridge."

In addition to Farron Ridge, Shipman had been working on several other marketing proposals to present to U.S. Tobacco, including the introduction of a high-end champagne. The champagne proposal had been in the same stack as the Farron Ridge proposal when Shipman accompanied Opdycke back to Connecticut. Before Opdycke and Shipman left Seattle for Connecticut, Opdycke told Shipman that they would present the champagne proposal if there was time. But the proposal was never presented, and when they returned to Seattle, Shipman approached Opdycke.

"We've got to do this champagne project," Shipman said, "and I should be in charge of it." Opdycke, however, told Shipman the champagne proposal was not big enough to interest U.S. Tobacco. But Shipman wasn't willing to give up. The more he thought about the idea, the more he liked it, so in his spare time, he developed a business plan to start his own champagne winery.

While Shipman worked on his idea in the winter of 1978-1979, Opdycke's worst nightmare occurred. An arctic freeze crept into the Ste. Michelle vineyards and lingered for several days. Although the damage wouldn't be fully known until spring, the Ste. Michelle vineyardist had confided to Shipman that winery had been badly hurt. Shipman went back to the archives and dug up a report in which the vineyardist emphasized that before planting the vinifera vines, the hard pan—a layer of clay that separated the top soil from a layer of soil below—had to be ripped with a digger. According to the vineyardist, if the hard pan was not ripped, the grape vines would go down, hit the hard pan, and then spread, exposing the vines to a great risk of freezing. At the time, there was still a debate whether freezing was an issue. After reading the report, Shipman put the pieces of the puzzle together. The soil had not been ripped as recommended, and as it turned out, over half of Ste. Michelle's delicate vinifera vines died that winter.

Although the lost vines would not completely destroy the winery, Ste. Michelle would be disastrously short of product for the next three years. Shipman knew that Ste. Michelle would keep him around, but he questioned his career opportunities there.

In early 1980, Opdycke, who decided he needed a president for the company, hired Allen Shoup. In Shipman's estimation, Shoup had taken the best job in the company. From day one, Shipman had set his sights on becoming president of the company. Now Shoup had won the prize. Shipman realized that Shoup was more qualified. He had been a financial analyst for Chrysler, worked in brand development at Gallo, served as director of marketing for Max Factor, and had most recently been the chief of corporate communications for Boise Cascade.

For Shipman, the sting of Shoup's hiring lingered. He had left the East Coast to advance his career more quickly, but now it was stalling. Also, he believed his fate was now hitched to Allen Shoup's star. And Shoup was an unknown commodity. With the grapes frozen, Allen Shoup as his boss, and the champagne winery idea rejected, Shipman began to feel that his opportunities at Ste. Michelle were limited. He had been working on and off on the business plan for building a champagne winery for several months. It was time, he decided, to put his plan into action.

"Being an entrepreneur," Shipman would later admit, "isn't something that I was drawn to do. The bottom line is that entrepreneurs are what they are because they can't work for anybody else. It's not a choice. It's more like a curse. Running my own business was something I felt I had to do."

CHAPTER THREE

PERFECTING THE ART OF BOREDOM

IN HIS EARLY TWENTIES, Gordon Bowker dreamed of becoming a writer. But he gave up the dream because it was too hard. Instead, he became a reluctant, yet highly successful businessman. Bowker was the consummate idea man—an abstract thinker with incredible instincts to anticipate market trends years before they unfolded. According to his friend and business associate Terry Heckler, with whom Bowker founded the ad agency Heckler Bowker, Bowker had an uncanny ability to sense societal needs based on his own needs.

"He needed a good cup of coffee," Heckler would later say about Bowker, "and he couldn't find it in Seattle, so he started Starbucks and made his own. He couldn't find a good beer he wanted to drink, so dammit, he started a brewery, and brewed his own."

Some said Bowker had the prescience to see around corners. Others claimed he had tremendous powers of observation and was able to combine seemingly unrelated pieces of information into a coherent business idea.

Bowker had a quiet, reflective demeanor, but his brain was constantly at work. He was always thinking, always writing. A keen observer of popular American culture, Bowker understood the psyche of the American people, and he learned through his experiences in advertising, how to tap into their desires, their insecurities, and their longing for a better, more authentic experience. But the real key to his success, according to Heckler, was that Bowker had perfected the art of boredom. Bowker, Heckler claimed, actually worked at being bored. It was Bowker's theory that if he was bored, good ideas—when they popped into his head—would have an opportunity to come forward and assert themselves.

By his own admission, he "liked to loaf." He had come of age in the 1960s and there was a rebellious, counterculture streak that ran dead center through the complexities of his personality. Bowker never sought to get rich with his business ventures. Instead, he started businesses to create social diversity and to make his life more interesting. There were times, however, when Bowker wondered if perhaps he started the businesses he did to replace something that was missing in his life.

He was born October 28, 1942, in Oakland, California. His father, Gordon Bowker Sr., was a Navy man in the submarine service who was killed that same year in the South Pacific by a Japanese depth charge. After his father's death, Bowker and his mother moved back to Seattle where he lived with his grandparents, the Ringseth's, in Ballard. His grandfather, Paul Ringseth, became one of the strongest influences in his life and Bowker, as an adult, would always wear a gold ring, which his grandfather gave him, with a gold nugget that Ringseth had extracted from the Yukon gold fields.

Ringseth, a Norwegian immigrant, came to the United States during the Alaska gold rush in the 1890s. A proponent of the "easy come, easy go" philosophy, Ringseth had started and folded various businesses during his life and he had made and lost several fortunes along the way. Among his many business ventures, Ringseth grub-staked miners, ran a stage line in Alaska, owned a construction business, and ran a grocery store in Seattle. By the time he was seventy, Ringseth was dead broke—without a pension or social security. But he did not bemoan his bad luck. Instead, he started a new business. While working for the state of Washington as a real estate inspector several years prior, he recognized there was an opportunity to make money teaching people to pass their real estate broker's examination, so he started a real estate school, the first of its kind in Washington State. He made a good living out of it and died, according to Bowker, a moderately wealthy man.

Bowker was a product of blended cultures. As a young boy in the 1940s, he grew up on Sunset Hill in Ballard, a middle-class Scandinavian neighborhood in Seattle where the economy was largely based on fishing. Many of the families on Bowker's block had fishing boats. The kids he grew up with had names such as Ingvar Carlsen, Paul Ackervic, or Ollie Iverson. When the kids in his neighborhood played hide-and-seek, rather than calling "Ollie Ollie Oxenfree," they called "Oly Oly Olsenfree."

"I didn't know I was Scandinavian," Bowker later admitted as an adult, "I thought that's just the way the world was."

In the 1950s, Bowker's mother married Green Berry Gillespie, a Boeing aeronautical engineer. Bowker was uprooted from the Scandinavian fishing culture and immersed into the world of aerospace and aeronautics. He spent his teenage years in Burien, a suburb south of Seattle that was heavily populated with Boeing employees. To Bowker, it seemed that everyone he knew in Burien had a father who was somehow associated with Boeing or the burgeoning airline industry, either as pilots, engineers, or airline mechanics.

Bowker was extremely bright, but never excelled in school. He simply wasn't interested in subjects that didn't relate to his life. He attended O'Dea High, a private Catholic high school in Seattle. The culture at O'Dea, he later recalled, was based on corporal punishment. For entertainment, Bowker and his classmates bated the Irish Christian brothers to incite them to violence. It was, according to Bower, an "us versus them mentality."

In 1960, Bowker graduated from O'Dea. He decided to attend the University of San Francisco. In 1962, the World's Fair was held in Seattle. During the summer, Bowker met two students from Emmanuel College in Cambridge, England. They were hitchhiking their way across the United States and they had come to Seattle for the World's Fair. The two hitchhikers invited Bowker to visit them in England. Rather than return for his junior year of college, Bowker took them up on their offer. He and a friend bought EuroRail passes and spent a year wandering through Europe by train.

He began his European travels with a three-week stay at Emmanuel College, where he discovered the social system was based on the consumption of liquids. At Emmanuel, they drank coffee all morning, tea all afternoon, and beer all night. Bowker thought the Nescafe coffee in Cambridge tasted awful, but the beer was a completely different story. There was a pub across the street from Emmanuel called the Fountain and each night Bowker and his friends at Emmanuel closed it down. The beer served at the Fountain was a bitter ale from the Greene King Brewery in Suffolk County, England, and while most Americans accused English beer of being warm and flat, Bowker loved the distinctive taste of the bittering hops that characterized the warm English ale.

By the winter of 1962, Bowker had wandered south to Rome, where he rented a room in a pension on the Piazza Fontana Trevi. One day, while sitting at a cafe reading the *Rome Daily American*, he ordered a cappuccino. Without looking up from the newspaper, he took a sip, and was shocked that it actually tasted good. It was a revelation. He had never consumed coffee for the taste. Rather, he had always drunk coffee for stimulation and as part of a social ritual. Bowker filed the discovery away in the back of his mind: it was possible to drink coffee that tasted good.

Bowker returned to the University of San Francisco in the fall of 1963 and resumed his studies in political science. In his senior year, 1965, he became editor of the *Foghorn*, the university paper. Editing the *Foghorn*, according to Bowker, was one of the most exhilarating experiences of his life. It was a watershed year in American politics. Students protested the Vietnam War on campuses across the country.

Martin Luther King led civil rights demonstrators from Selma to Montgomery, Alabama. The Watts race riots erupted in Los Angeles, and at nearby Berkeley, the Free Speech Movement was in full swing. Instead of going to class, Bowker devoted his efforts, full-time, to putting out the *Foghorn*. His grades went to hell, but he didn't care. School had no meaning or consequence to him. In the spirit of the times, he quit eight credits shy of graduation and returned to Seattle.

He got an apartment on Capitol Hill in Seattle and lived a hand-to-mouth existence. He drove a taxi and worked part-time as a guide for Seattle's underground tours in Pioneer Square, leading tourist through a series of basements that were formed when the city of Seattle was built on top of the rubble caused by the great fire of 1889. It was a confusing time for Bowker. He had no clear vision of where his life was heading.

In 1968, Bowker decided to make a serious run at being a writer and landed a contract writing educational films for a subsidiary of King Broadcasting called King Screen Productions. The work led to a full-time writing position at *Seattle* magazine, a glossy, liberal, monthly publication affiliated with King Broadcasting.

Bowker wrote restaurant reviews and off-beat features about subjects as varied as cab driving and Catholic school. According to his friend and fellow writer, David Brewster, Bowker was an oddity at *Seattle* magazine. He was the only writer on staff who was born in Seattle and he hadn't attended an Ivy League school like the majority of the staff. Years after he left *Seattle* magazine, Bowker confided to Brewster that he always felt as though he was on probation while he was there.

For Bowker, feelings of insecurity were a small price to pay for a steady income. After receiving his first paycheck, Bowker asked himself what he wanted to do now that he was making real money. His instant reaction was that he didn't want to drink any more bad coffee. But Bowker couldn't find good coffee in Seattle, so he expanded his search to Vancouver, Canada, where he located a coffee roaster called Murchie's. In the summer of 1969, Bowker drove to Murchie's—then a

mom-and-pop store that had survived mainly on their tea business—
and brought a couple pounds of Melitta grind across the border.

Within short order, he was making a trip to Murchie's about once
a month, each time bringing back increasing amounts of coffee.
Eventually his Alfa Romeo took on the permanent smell of coffee.
And the custom agents at the U.S.-Canadian border started giving
him curious looks when he told them he was bringing back twenty
pounds of coffee.

His friends' reactions to his gourmet coffee were varied. Some
thought he had an abnormal coffee fetish. But others really liked it
and asked if he could get them some the next time he went to
Vancouver. One day in the winter of 1971, Bowker was on the return
leg of one of his coffee runs, when the idea for Starbucks Coffee came
to him. He was heading south on Interstate 5, and the sun was low
on the horizon as he came alongside Lake Samish south of Belling-
ham. The sun glinted off the lake and blasted him in the face.

"I felt like Saul at Tarsus," Bowker would later recall, referring to
the apostle Paul, known as Saul of Tarsus, who rode a horse on the road
to Damascus when he was struck by lightning, knocked off his horse,
and transformed into a Christian zealot. The idea for Starbuck's came
to him in a flash. I don't need to go to Vancouver to buy coffee, Bowker
thought—I can start my own coffee business in Seattle.

Bowker was convinced that people in the Seattle area would pay
a premium price for quality, roasted coffee. It was Bowker's theory
that American food and beverage companies had been progressively
making taste decisions based on economics. Over the years, coffee
companies had resorted to a number of strategies to reduce their costs.
They not only started buying cheaper coffee, they also roasted it
lighter, taking the moisture out of it so it weighed less, which reduced
the cost of goods. Perhaps there was no perceptible difference in taste
at each adjustment, but cumulatively, Bowker believed, there was a
huge difference.

Later that winter, *Seattle* folded, leaving Bowker without a job.
The situation motivated him to start two businesses, Starbucks Coffee

and Heckler Bowker, an advertising and design firm. Bowker proposed the idea of starting a coffee business to his friends Jerry Baldwin and Zev Siegl one afternoon while the three sat on the lawn behind a house he was renting at the foot of West Bertona Avenue in Seattle.

Neither Siegl nor Baldwin were businessmen, but both were eager to start a business. Siegl was a history teacher, Baldwin taught English at a broadcast school. It was okay to be poor when they were young, Siegl had once told Baldwin, but he didn't want to be poor when he was old. At the time when Bowker approached Baldwin and Siegl with his idea, the two had already been toying with several ideas of their own.

Baldwin and Siegl found Bowker's idea appealing, and Siegl soon traveled to the Bay Area in California to research coffee companies. Siegl located Peet's Coffee and Tea Company in Berkeley. Its owner, Alfred Peet, was a Dutchman who had spent his life in the coffee business. Peet, who had a passionate love for good coffee, as well as coffee connections all over the world, was highly supportive of the trio's efforts and agreed to be their supplier until they could get their own roaster.

With the support of Alfred Peet behind them, Baldwin, Bowker, and Siegl agreed to put in $1,500 apiece to start the business. They got another $5,000 through a loan from Seafirst Bank. The loan, Bowker later recalled, was a setup job. Siegl's brother-in-law introduced the trio to his personal lawyer, John Ryan, who invited them to have lunch at his home in the wealthy Highlands neighborhood of Seattle. During lunch, Ryan listened to the their plans for a coffee company, and then sent them to his friend Sid Imus, a manager of a Seafirst Bank branch. The threesome made a one-hour presentation to Sid Imus and another Seafirst banker, Barrett Worthington. Baldwin later admitted that "it was absolute amateur hour." Their business plan, prepared by Baldwin, was a one-page, hand-written balance sheet on accounting paper. But at the end of the presentation, Imus told them that they had their $5,000 loan.

To Baldwin, it seemed almost too easy, but that was business in Seattle in the early 1970s. Bowker loved it. You could start a small business with modest resources. You didn't have to capitalize, and best of all, you didn't have to talk to investment bankers and listen to their ideas about why your business wouldn't work. "Me and my friends would just say let's do this," Bowker would recall, "and we did. In the 1970s, Seattle was a different place than it is today. Back then it was cowboy."

Baldwin, a San Francisco native who transplanted to Seattle, thought of Seattle as the boondocks—especially in terms of food sophistication. At the time, there were few fine restaurants and most establishments served generic continental cuisine. The clubs in downtown Seattle, Baldwin lamented, closed at midnight on Saturday. Seattle was a bizarre place, Baldwin concluded, but it provided fertile ground for starting food related businesses.

Baldwin, Siegl, and Bowker divided the duties necessary to open Starbucks. Bowker, now that he was an advertising executive, was given the task of naming the company. Bowker turned to his partner Terry Heckler for help. Heckler believed that words that began with the consonants *st* were strong words, because of the word *strong*, so Bowker made a list of *st* words. Then Heckler researched the names of turn-of-the century mining camps on Mt. Rainier and discovered the name *Starbo*. When Bowker heard *Starbo*, he immediately thought of Starbuck, the first mate in Herman Melville's classic novel *Moby Dick*. The name *Starbucks,* he believed, was a perfect fit.

For the Starbucks' logo, Heckler browsed through old marine books and found a picture of sixteenth-century Norse woodcut—a seductive bare-breasted mermaid holding her tail fins aloft. The logo, they hoped, would be as enticing as the coffee.

In April of 1971, Siegl, Baldwin, and Bowker opened the first Starbucks store on Western and Virginia in the Pike Place Market in Seattle and sold roasted coffee supplied by Alfred Peet. Their timing was hardly ideal. For the past three years, Boeing had been slashing its workforce. Thousands fled the city. Homes were abandoned. In the same month that Starbucks opened, a billboard appeared on

Highway 509—the highway that led to Boeing's factories—that read: "Will the last person leaving Seattle please turn out the lights?"

Despite the ailing Seattle economy, Starbucks racked up $49,000 worth of sales in their first nine months of business. The partners considered the business a moderate success. Siegl was the only paid employee. Baldwin kept the books, and Bowker helped out at the store on weekends. Within a year after the opening, Peet informed the partners that Starbucks was getting too big and arranged for them to purchase a roaster in Holland. Starbucks rented a ramshackle warehouse in Seattle's Fisherman's Terminal where they planned to set up their makeshift roasting plant. The roaster, as it turned out, arrived in parts—without a manual—in an open container, and Baldwin had a friend of his, a fisherman, put it together. Later in 1972, Starbucks opened a second store in University Village in Seattle. A third store followed in 1976.

Before starting Starbucks, Bowker had asked a variety of people what they thought of his idea for a store that sold fresh, deep-roasted coffee. Many, including his friend David Brewster, who often met Bowker for lunch, told him it was a stupid idea. Bowker would later tell Brewster that the greatest pleasure in his life was to have an idea that all kinds of smart people said was stupid, and have it turn out successful.

A few years later, Brewster would have his own idea—to start a weekly newspaper, which he talked about each time he and Bowker had lunch. Bowker finally got so tired of hearing Brewster talk about starting a weekly newspaper, that he told him he wasn't going to have lunch with him again until he did something about it. Perhaps it was the impetus Brewster needed, because in 1976, he launched an alternative newspaper called the *Seattle Weekly*. Bowker invested $5,000 in the venture and wrote the first restaurant review for the paper under the pseudonym Lars Henry Ringseth. Brewster was continually amazed by the torture Bowker went through as a writer. Bowker was a slow, agonized writer—a craftsman who sweated over every word. Each draft, and their were often many, was on a different color paper. But the result, according to Brewster, was always great.

After Starbucks opened, Bowker removed himself from day-to-day affairs so he could concentrate on the ad agency Heckler Bowker, which was busy handling the K2 ski account. From the start, Heckler Bowker was an avant-garde ad agency that was years ahead of its time. Jerry Baldwin, Bowker's life-long friend and business partner, once made the observation that the key to Bowker's success was his ability to partner with people whose skills complemented his own. The partnership of Bowker and Heckler was certainly a living testimony to Baldwin's observation.

Heckler had studied fine arts at Carnegie Mellon University in Pittsburgh and had gone on to earn a Master's in Communication from the University of Waterloo in Ontario. Heckler was cerebral, highly intelligent, and had incredible artistic skills. "At the same time," according to Bowker, "he had a certain dyslexic aspect to his thought process, so that what came out of the hopper was usually something unique and unusual."

Bowker, for his part, continually surprised Heckler with what he produced. There was a richness in Bowker's writing that Heckler rarely saw in the ad world. This richness, Heckler maintained, came from Bowker's encyclopedic knowledge base, acquired through voracious reading, coupled with his amazing ability to retain what he learned. Bowker, the former newspaper editor, was a compulsive reader of newspapers. Anywhere that Heckler and Bowker traveled outside of Seattle, Bowker had to read the newspaper from that place. A newspaper, Heckler came to believe, was a permanent fixture under Bowker's arm.

From the start, Heckler Bowker was guided by Heckler's basic philosophy that advertising didn't work. Heckler and Bowker took a novel approach to capturing the consumer's attention, creating ads that shook up the traditional relationship of art to copy. For the K2 ski account, they produced ads without copy, and ads with copy that wasn't related to the art. One advertisement was a takeoff on the old chewing tobacco ads that were painted on the sides of barns. Heckler and Bowker hired an artist to paint the slogan "Chew K2" on a barn in the Skagit Valley, an agricultural area in Washington. They ran the photo in ski publications without any copy to accompany it.

Heckler and Bowker were young, arrogant, and convinced they were right. They also had high standards and weren't willing to accept the fact that just because they were in Seattle, they had to compromise their integrity. Their bravado carried them a long way. In the winter of 1973, Heckler Bowker's K2 ads caught the eye of Jim Foster, the advertising director for the Rainier Brewing Company in Seattle. When Foster inquired who had done the ads, he was surprised to discover they were done by a Seattle agency, Heckler Bowker.

Foster was looking for unique advertising agencies that could help redefine Rainier's blue-collar image. He believed that unusual advertising was the only way that Rainier could distinguish itself in a stagnant beer market. Rainier's advertising was traditional of the early 1970s. Their flagship product, Rainier Beer, was a mainstream lager that was presented in television and radio advertisements as a reward for a hard day's work or something to enjoy after leisure activities. Bowker called the Rainier commercials "macho reward spots." The ad campaign, developed by McCann Erickson, featured the slogan "Rainier's got the flavor when you've got a thirst for life."

The campaign was targeted at young consumers between twenty-one and thirty-five, a market segment that Rainier's research had shown represented not only the largest share of the market, but also the market segment that they could convert most easily to their brand. The campaign, however, had failed to have any meaningful effect. Prior to McCann Erickson, Rainier had employed several hot New York agencies, but none of their campaigns ever translated into a gain in market share.

In 1973, Rainier Beer was second in market share in Washington State, trailing the leader, Olympia Beer, by a significant margin. The big three breweries, Anheuser-Busch, Miller, and Schlitz, were expanding their presence in Washington State with increased advertising, and Anheuser-Busch, in particular, was beginning to move up rapidly in market share. The big three were not yet a major factor in Washington, but Foster believed it was only a matter of time before Rainier felt the icy chill of competition from the national breweries.

On Foster's recommendation, Jim Martin, Rainier's director of marketing, arranged to meet Heckler and Bowker at their offices on Capitol Hill in Seattle. Heckler Bowker, located on the second floor of a house, had cramped offices that were converted bedrooms. The meeting was held in Bowker's office, and Martin, Foster, Heckler, and Bowker huddled around a table.

Several minutes into the meeting, as Foster gravely explained Rainier's situation, the closet door opened in Bowker's office and Jerry Baldwin stepped out. It was so cramped that Foster and Martin were forced to stand up to let him by.

"Don't mind Jerry," Bowker told them. "That's his office."

Foster and Martin couldn't believe that Bowker was renting Baldwin the closet as an office, so they walked over and opened the closet door. Sure enough, it was Baldwin's office, consisting of a chair, table, and typewriter underneath a naked light bulb.

Foster and Martin left the meeting thinking that Bowker and Heckler were impressive, but highly unusual. "They had a unique way of seeing things," Foster would later recall, "and they weren't effected by convention in any sense of the word."

Heckler Bowker's first assignment for Rainier was the redesign of Rainier Ale's packaging. Heckler maintained that it was merely a test to see if they could meet deadlines. Pleased with the results of the Rainier Ale project, Foster and Martin asked Heckler and Bowker to take a look at their main label, Rainier Beer. To help acquaint Heckler and Bowker with Rainier, Foster arranged a tour of the brewery.

On the morning the tour was scheduled, Bowker woke up running on three cylinders, but Heckler convinced him to take the tour. During the tour, Bowker, Heckler, and the Rainier executives moved between rooms of different temperatures. As they entered a refrigerated room, Bowker fainted into Heckler's arms. The Rainier executives hovered over Bowker, attempting to revive him. Several nervous minutes ticked by before Bowker was able to sit up.

Later, driving back to their offices with Heckler, Bowker said, "I guess they'll never forget that meeting."

That, in Heckler's mind, was vintage Bowker. Bowker had a flair for the dramatic. He was the master of surprise. Heckler always believed that Bowker enjoyed embarrassing him, but Bowker wasn't trying to embarrass Heckler at all. He was just doing what came naturally to him. At the beginning of Seattle SuperSonics basketball games, Bowker, who stood next to Heckler, poked out his chest and sang the "Star Spangled Banner" at the top his lungs. He would sing so loud and proud, according to Heckler, that people would turn around to see who it was that was making such a racket. Or on business flights, Bowker would recite the complimentary prayer out loud, just to remind Continental of their great social insight.

To advertise Rainier Beer, Bowker and Heckler formulated a strategy for Rainier that was based on one central idea: As Heckler would later describe it, "get on TV and make each commercial as different as possible." They devised a campaign that featured a series of wacky TV spots, each one totally different, unique, and unpredictable. They wanted their ads to be conversation pieces, so that one person would see a Rainier commercial and say to another: "Hey did you see that Rainier commercial about the frogs?" and the other person would say, "No, I saw the commercial with the Rainier Beer containers crossing the road." Bowker and Heckler also wanted the commercials to be fun, so that people would think that Rainier was a fun company, and thus produced a beer that was fun to drink.

When Heckler and Bowker pitched their ideas to Foster and Martin, the two Rainier executives laughed out loud. They left the meeting in shock, and as they walked away from Heckler Bowker's offices, Foster told Martin that he thought the campaign could well save the company.

Initially, Heckler and Bowker produced five thirty-second commercials for Rainier, each commercial completely different than the other. One featured a couple driving on a mountain road who came upon a Beer Crossing sign, only to discover a herd of life-size legged Rainier Beer bottles suddenly darting across the road. It rained the day the commercial was scheduled to be filmed and according to Heckler, the Rainier executives wanted to cancel the shoot. Bowker and Heckler, however, convinced them to continue. This was Washington, they insisted, and it was supposed to rain, so they improvised the dialog on the spot and shot the commercial in the rain through the *twap, twap, twap* of the car windshield wipers.

Heckler Bowker did four other spots: in one, frogs on a mountain pond croaked "Rainier"; in another, a whistling lady who looked like Liberace sat at a piano. Two other commercials were spoofs of *Casablanca*. The commercials created an overnight sensation. Rainier's distributors loved them. Within six months, Rainier saw a dramatic increase in sales and their telephone research found that recall and reaction to the new advertising was off the charts.

The highlight of the Rainier commercials came in 1974. Heckler and Bowker had developed a certain science that they applied to the Rainier commercials. They were usually parodies of someone or something that was prominent in the media. For one commercial, they proposed a parody of a popular television show, *The American Sportsman*, which featured a celebrity out hunting with a sports hero.

Part of the science that Heckler and Bowker applied to Rainier Beer commercials was to use people who'd been in the limelight and had fallen out of it. For the sports hero, Bowker and Heckler got Boom Boom Kirkman, a Seattle heavyweight fighter who had once been, but no longer was, prominent. For the celebrity, Foster suggested Mickey Rooney, who at the time was on the downside of his career and was appearing in a play in Seattle called *Three Goats and a Blanket*. Foster contacted Rooney through Rooney's agent, who later told Foster that Rooney would be willing to meet him at the hotel in Seattle where Rooney was staying.

At the meeting, Foster told Rooney about the commercial he had in mind. When Rooney asked what Foster was willing to pay, Foster humbly admitted that Rainier was a small brewery with a limited budget and could only afford to pay him $2,500.

"Rooney wouldn't do a commercial for $2,500 dollars," Rooney trumpeted, referring to himself in the third person. "Rooney will only accept $3,000."

Rainier paid Rooney $3,000. After shooting the commercial, Bowker drove Rooney out to an auto dealership on Aurora Avenue, where Rooney used the $3,000 to purchase a station wagon, which he used to drive home to California.

Rooney's celebrity put Rainier on the map and marked a turning point in an already successful campaign. The commercial was one of the most successful spots Rainier had ever run. Based on the commercial's success, Rainier asked Rooney to shoot several more commercials, for which he was paid considerably more money.

Bowker's favorite Mickey Rooney ancedote happened one day when he was driving Rooney back to the Kennedy Hotel in Seattle after a day of shooting an American Sportsman commercial at Seattle's Discovery Park. Rooney, who was sitting in the back seat of the car, told Bowker he had a nag (horse) running at Yakima Meadows (a racetrack) and wondered where he could get a racing form.

Bowker drove down Third Avenue and stopped at a newstand at the corner of Third and Pike, where he purchased a racing form for Rooney. When he got back in the car, he handed the form to Rooney, who buried his head in the form as Bowker resumed driving. As the car neared the downtown Post Office, traffic was stopped by a group of socialist demonstrators chanting into bullhorns. As Bowker would recall, "Here's Mickey Rooney—star of stage, screen, and television— kissed Judy Garland—and he looks up from his racing form, unrolls the window, leans out and yells at the top of his lungs: 'Why don't you bums get jobs?'"

Rooney, according to Bowker, had ideas a "mile-a-minute." He talked constantly about plans he had for businesses. One was Mickey

Rooney Macaroni. Another was Thirst, a licorice-flavored soft drink. He had also written an ad that he planned to pitch to Lavoris mouthwash that he called The Lavoris Chorus. It featured an entire chorus of people gargling. Rooney was always pitching ideas to Foster. He told Foster he could come back for the summer and do a Pro-Am golf tournament called the Rooney Rainier Open. "Rooney Rainier, R, R," Rooney said to Foster. "Do you get it?" As entertainment, Rooney suggested they could have Mickey Rooney and his dancing wives.

In four years, based largely on Heckler Bowker's commercials, Rainier became the number one selling beer in Washington State and one of the most prominent regional breweries in the United States. Ultimately, Heckler Bowker produced up to two hundred and eighty commercials for Rainier. Eventually, the commercials became so popular that the Seattle media would turn up each year to cover the filming.

By 1976, however, Bowker had begun to dislike the advertising business. He was tired of what he called "flacking" for other people's products. Bowker sold his shares of Heckler Bowker (which then became Heckler and Associates) and went into semiretirement. He spent several years, as he described it, "just floating." Some days he picked blackberries in Seattle's Discovery Park. Bowker had a particular love for the true Northwest wild blackberries—the small ones that come out in June and July—and he would pack himself a lunch with two Ballantine Ales in a knapsack and go into the bush and pick wild blackberries all morning. When he got tired, he would spread out his lunch on a blanket and sip his ale, enjoying its distinctive, oaky flavor.

Heckler would not allow Bowker to bask in his boredom for long. In 1980, he recruited Bowker to coordinate the activities for K2 at the Winter Olympics in Lake Placid, New York. It was a frustrating project for Bowker. As part of the promotional effort, they were producing a video for the Mahre brothers, Steve and Phil, the Olympic skiers from Washington State. Unfortunately, the weather for the 1980 Olympics was not only bad for ski racing, but also for shooting video and Bowker looked forward to the end of the project.

As the Olympics came to a close, people began to ask Bowker what he was going to do next. By that time, Bowker had made a conscious effort to tell people that he was going to start a brewery. He'd been successful with coffee, why not try beer, he mused. Bowker figured that if he told enough people that he was going to start a brewery, he'd be obligated to do it. Otherwise, he'd have to listen to all the people he told, who would come back to him with comments such as: "Hey Gordon, what about that brewery you said you were starting?"

Bowker had been mulling over the idea of starting a brewery for several years. In the late 1970s, he had read a newsletter about the first American microbrewery called New Albion in California that was started by Jack McAuliffe. Bowker found the idea of a microbrewery interesting. It sounded Bowkeresque—modest and against the grain. He wondered why more people hadn't done what McAuliffe had at New Albion.

After the Olympics, Bowker began to research microbreweries in the U.S. Visiting the Boulder Brewery in Boulder, Colorado, he was surprised to discover it was a true cottage industry. The tiny homebrew establishment was located in a shed on a goat farm and the owners made their own wooden cases.

Bowker also visited the Anchor Brewery in San Francisco. Anchor, which produced Anchor Steam Beer, was run by Fritz Maytag, considered the godfather of microbrewing. Bowker also attended a microbrewery seminar sponsored by Fritz Maytag, and during the seminar, Maytag told the group that his dream was that someday in the future, he would be able to go to different cities in the U. S. and find that each city had its own brewery. Bowker shared Maytag's dream.

While Bowker conducted informal microbrewery research, he also worked on the Farron Ridge project with Shipman at Ste. Michelle. According to Bowker, Ste. Michelle at the time had a hierarchy of executives in fancy offices and expensive suites, but as he looked at the company and watched it work, it appeared to him that Shipman was the guy that did all the work. As Bowker saw it, everything would get passed down from desk to desk and end up on Shipman's desk. Clearly impressed with Shipman's capabilities, Bowker decided that Shipman would be a good partner for his new venture, so he invited him to dinner at the Adriatica, a new, upscale restaurant on the western side of Seattle's Lake Union.

Bowker created an aura of suspense by not telling Shipman what he wanted to talk about at dinner. It was a trick he had learned in the advertising business. Rather than presenting the offer to Shipman ad hoc, Bowker wanted the proper amount of time and the right place to make a complete presentation to Shipman.

In the past, Shipman had informally pitched Bowker on the idea of starting a champagne winery, but could never accurately gauge Bowker's reaction to the idea. He knew the wheels were spinning in Bowker's mind, he just couldn't tell in what direction. Consequently, Shipman guessed that Bowker had invited him to dinner to talk about the winery, or maybe to offer him a job at Starbucks.

But that night over dinner at the Adriatica, Bowker told Shipman that instead of opening a champagne winery, he was thinking of opening a microbrewery. "The only thing is," Bowker said, "I've got to find somebody to be president."

"I want to be president," Shipman boomed before Bowker even had a chance to make the offer. Later, Shipman would admit that he felt as though he'd been hypnotized for a long time and Bowker had said the magic words to make him bark like a dog.

The dream to open the brewery, according to Shipman, had been there all along. It was just waiting to be activated. The irony of the situation was not lost on Shipman. During his college days, when he wanted to enter the beer business, Bob Taylor had convinced him to go into wine industry instead. Now here he was ready to open a champagne winery, and Bowker was convincing him to start a brewery. Shipman had come full circle.

As Bowker later remembered the evening: "I had never thought of offering the presidency to Paul as part of my agenda. I asked Paul to dinner because I wanted to interest him in the idea and get his participation. If I had thought it through, I would have thought that he would be the ideal person to be president. But I didn't know that the conversation was going to necessarily head in that direction. But when Paul said in his booming voice that he wanted to be president, I was elated and relieved. 'Good, I thought. I couldn't do this myself. Now we're off and running.'"

CHAPTER FOUR

TRUE ALE

BOWKER TRUSTED HIS INSTINCTS. But Shipman wanted statistical proof that a market opportunity existed for locally brewed beer, so he poured through volumes of research publications about the beer market. Shipman liked what he saw in the numbers. Import beers, statistics showed, were the fastest growing segment of the U.S. beer market—and Seattle drank more import beers than most other U. S. cities. If the import beer market continued to grow at that rate, Shipman calculated, they could operate a brewery profitably by capturing only 1 percent of the import beer market in Seattle.

Shipman was committed to the idea of starting a brewery, but he wasn't willing to give up the security of his job at Ste. Michelle, so he and Bowker maintained daily phone contact to discuss their business plans. From the start, Shipman and Bowker were in complete agreement about the type of ale they would brew. It would be a premium-quality English-style ale that was freshly brewed, locally produced, and competitive in both taste and price with the best-selling imported beers and ales.

Freshness, Bowker and Shipman believed, would be their key advantage. Imports suffered taste and freshness degradation from the rigors of long-distance shipping, and many imports had their formulas altered for export to stabilize the product's shelf life or to satisfy laws restricting alcohol percentages. But a locally brewed keg beer, distributed immediately to nearby taverns, would offer beer drinkers a fresh product, without taste degradation, that was free of stabilizing additives.

Bowker, perhaps more than Shipman, understood the importance of freshness. He had identified a movement in food and beverage products that he called *connoisumerism*. Sophisticated consumers, Bowker believed, were turning away from mass-marketed, freeze-dried products in favor of those that were fresh and locally produced. They cared about the ingredients, they cared about freshness, and they cared about the product's origin. Bowker believed that these connoisumers were looking for a more authentic experience in the products that they consumed.

In the course of his microbrewery research, Bowker had read about the Campaign for Real Ale, a consumer movement that swept through England in the early '70s, and Bowker believed that Americans shared a similar desire for authentic ale.

In England, cask conditioning of draft beer had long been a tradition, but with the growth of national brewing groups and the modernization efforts of the '50s through the '70s, the convenience of marketing pasteurized and filtered keg ale was diminishing British brewers' interest in cask-conditioned ale.

Cask-conditioned ale was labor intensive. It was shipped by the brewer with some residual sugar and living yeast in the barrel, causing the ale to undergo a secondary fermentation process. The result was a fresh, living ale, with natural carbonation in the cask. But the problem with real ale, and the reason for its decline, was that each cask of living ale needed to be monitored for clarity, natural carbonation, and palate.

In 1971, a group of drinking buddies in Britain decided to start a consumer campaign to save real ale. The group, which included several journalists, struck a nerve with the beer-drinking British public and sparked a national consumer movement. The Campaign for Real

Ale (CAMRA) started a monthly newspaper called *What's Brewing* and wrote a paperback bestseller, *The Good Beer Guide,* that identified pubs that served the best cask-conditioned ales. At its height, CAMRA had more than 25,000 members and was generally credited with saving cask-conditioned ale in Britain. Equally important, CAMRA showed British brewers, dominated by the big six (Bass, Allied Breweries, Whitbread, Watney, Courage, and Scottish and Newcastle) that consumers were willing to fight back to preserve the quality and freshness of their beer.

To learn more about ale, Bowker and Shipman devoured *The World Guide to Beer,* a book by London-based writer Michael Jackson. In his book, Jackson included a family tree of beer that was divided at the trunk into two main categories: top-fermenting beers and bottom-fermenting beers. Ales were top-fermenting beers. Lagers were bottom-fermenting beers. The true point of distinction was that ales were fermented with a yeast strain—*Saccharomyces cerevisiae*—that floated to the top of the beer during fermentation, while lagers were made with a yeast strain—*Saccharomyces carlsbergensis* that sank to the bottom.

Bowker, it seemed to Shipman, was obsessed with the concept of true ale. Bowker had learned that breweries in the United States did not always adhere to Jackson's definition of an ale. In the States, a beer could be labeled as an ale whether or not it used an ale yeast. All that was required was that the beer be fermented at a warm temperature. Bowker discovered that many ales in the United States, including Rainier Ale, were actually made with a lager yeast. Thus, they were not true ales. In Bowker's opinion, true ale was a marketable point of distinction. Their brewery, he insisted, would brew a true ale, fermented with the *Saccharomyces cerevisiae* yeast strain.

The process of top fermentation with ale yeast had its roots in the earliest days of brewing—when the workings of fermentation were not completely understood and refrigeration was nonexistent. Ale yeast fermented beer at room temperatures—55 to 70 degrees Fahrenheit—making it ideal for brewing in preindustrial societies. The difficulty with top fermentation, however, was the susceptibility of the yeast to breed with naturally occurring yeasts in the atmosphere. This often caused wild fermentations.

By the 1850s, French scientist Louis Pasteur had begun to develop a real understanding of yeast. By then it was known that some brewers' yeast rose to the top of the fermentation vessel while others sank to the bottom, although no one was sure why. Eventually, a Bavarian yeast was broken down to a single strain by Emil Hansen in Carlsberg, Denmark. This bottom-fermenting yeast came to be known as *Saccharomyces carlsbergensis*. Later, Bavarian brewers would observe that beer made with the *Saccharomyces carlsbergensis* yeast would become progressively more stable when stored in icy alpine caves during the summer. This observation led them to seek colder and longer fermentation periods, followed by several months of maturation in almost freezing conditions.

Lager beer required cold temperatures for fermentation and storage, but it offered several advantages over ale. Lagers not only tasted cleaner, they were also more stable, because bacteria can't propagate as easily in cold temperatures. This meant that lager beers could be stored for longer periods of time. Refrigeration, developed in the 1880s, furthered the popularity of lager beer. With refrigeration, beer could be mass-produced in a central location and then shipped long distances without spoiling.

In colonial America, the brewing style had been mainly English, consisting of various ales and porters. But in 1840, a Bavarian brewer named Johann Wagner brought a bottom-fermenting yeast from Munich and opened a brewery in Philadelphia. Wagner was soon followed by a wave of German immigrants, many of them brewers, who brought with them a taste for German lager. By 1860, the majority of the beer brewed in the United States was lager, and more than a century later, lager's dominance of the American brewing landscape would remain unchallenged.

Brewing an English ale in America seemed a risky proposition. After all, American beer drinkers had been conditioned by the big breweries, such as Anheuser-Busch and Miller, to like the taste of lager. Many people told Bowker and Shipman that their plan to brew an English-style ale was foolish. But Bowker, in particular, was accustomed to hearing that type of feedback. He'd been told, years earlier, that starting a gourmet coffee company was a stupid idea too.

Bowker and Shipman were also encouraged by the success of two English ales in Seattle. Watney's, sold in kegs, was doing well in Seattle taverns, and Charlie Finkel, former vice president of marketing at Ste. Michelle, had achieved great success in Seattle selling bottles of Old Brewery Pale Ale from the Samuel Smith brewery in Yorkshire.

Bowker and Shipman were confident that they could persuade Seattleites to drink a locally produced English-style ale. But before they could begin selling their ale, they first had to build a brewery and brew the beer. And neither one of them knew the first thing about building a brewery or brewing beer.

For inspiration and guidance, they turned to Fritz Maytag, owner of the Anchor Brewing Company in San Francisco. Anchor was arguably the last specialty brewery in America, and the smallest, when Maytag rescued the brewery from certain closure. His involvement with Anchor dated back to 1965 when he was a literature student at Stanford University. One day Maytag was sitting at a bar in San Francisco, sipping an Anchor Steam beer, when he was told that the Anchor Brewery was due to close at the end of the week. Maytag, whose grandfather had started the Iowa washing machine company, sold off a portion of his inherited Maytag stock to become a partner in the brewery.

Anchor's steam beer style was uniquely American and dated from the time when lager replaced ale as the primary beer style in the United States. Warm weather and lack of refrigeration in San Francisco led to the development of a technique in which lager yeasts were used, but fermentation was left to occur at warm temperatures more suitable for ale. This hybrid fermentation method produced a lively beer that released a burst of carbon dioxide when the keg was tapped. Hence the name *steam beer*.

Maytag later became Anchor's owner, and the brewery became his labor of love. Reviving the brewery was an uphill battle. It was located beneath a freeway, employed only one person, used baker's yeast, and brewed only draft beer. Maytag made all the deliveries himself. He once told a reporter that he was in the business of making a beer that most people didn't like. Maytag eventually upgraded the brewery by investing in a new brewhouse and improved the taste of the beer by using only high-quality ingredients such as whole hops, instead of hop pellets.

In 1975, Maytag moved his operation into the old Chase and Sanborn Coffee Factory on Potrero Hill in San Francisco. He transformed the building into one of the most handsome breweries in the country and by the early '80s, Anchor Steam—producing less than 10,000 barrels a year and serving mostly Bay Area accounts—had become a shining example of how a microbrewery could succeed in the United States.

In 1981, Shipman called Maytag and asked if he could tour the Anchor Steam Brewery. Maytag was more than willing to help Shipman. He spent an entire day with him, walking him through his brewery and giving him advice about the types of ingredients that he should use for his beer. Shipman was impressed. He had witnessed firsthand how Maytag's commitment to quality had translated into Anchor Steam's success. At the end of the day, Shipman decided he wanted to be just like Fritz Maytag.

Shipman took responsibility for writing the business plan for the new brewery. He worked on it in his office at Ste. Michelle during normal business hours. He could complete his daily duties at Ste. Michelle in two hours, so he normally spent the rest of the day working on the plan. If someone came into his office while he was writing the plan, he told them he was working on a secret project. He assumed no one knew what he was up to. But in the spring of 1981, Bowker called and told him that he had heard through the grapevine that the people at Ste. Michelle knew that he was working on a business plan for a microbrewery.

It was time for him to cut his ties with the winery, Bowker said. For Shipman, who had a wife and new baby at home, it was like jumping off a cliff. He was confident he would survive, but it was difficult to leave the security of Ste. Michelle. He told Bowker that he wasn't willing to leave his job at the winery until some seed money had been put down. The seed money would cover the cost of writing the prospectus. They would also use it to pay the lawyers, develop a name and label for the business and its product, and to secure a lease for a building. More importantly, the seed money would prove to Shipman that the venture was for real.

Shipman estimated that they needed about $5,000 to get started, but both he and Bowker were self-proclaimed tightwads who refused to invest their own money. Bowker, however, had a friend named Jerry Jones who would be willing to pony up the cash. But $5,000 didn't sound impressive enough for a high roller like Jones, so they decided to ask for $30,000 instead.

Bowker knew that Jones would invest in his idea. Bowker and Jones went back a long way. Jones had worked for Colorado ski resorts since the '60s, and in his various marketing roles at Sun Valley, Snowmass, and Keystone, he had used Heckler Bowker as his advertising agency. In the course of the working relationship, Bowker and Jones had become close friends. In 1973, Jones traveled to Seattle on business to meet with the K2 on nearby Vashon Island. During his stay, Bowker gave Jones a tour of the Pike Place Starbucks and their roasting plant in Fisherman's Terminal. After the tour, Bowker asked Jones to invest some money in the enterprise. Bowker offered Jones a big percentage of the company for $16,000, but at the time, Jones was in his early twenties and did not have a great deal of disposable income to risk. He also didn't see much promise in Starbucks, so he refused to invest.

Five Starbucks stores later—when the venture was showing signs of promise—Jones said if a similar deal ever presented itself, he wouldn't make the same mistake twice. So when Bowker called Jones and told him that he was starting a microbrewery, and then asked him for $30,000, Jones immediately agreed. He was selling a house in Keystone and would have extra cash available from the sale.

On May 4, Bowker and Shipman met with Jones at the Edgewater Hotel to sign the papers of incorporation for the Independent Ale Brewery, Inc. The meeting, at Bowker's behest, was held in the Jones' room—the room where John Lennon had stayed when the Beatles came to Seattle in the '60s. Ritualistic details, Shipman had come to discover, were very important to Bowker. Bowker and Shipman gave Jones a rundown of the business and presented him with the required documents. The statistics Shipman rattled off didn't make any sense to Jones, but he didn't care. He was betting on the abilities of Bowker and Shipman.

After signing the papers, Jones handed over a check for $10,000, with the understanding that Shipman and Bowker could draw on the remaining $20,000 as needed. In return, Jones was given 3,000 shares of common stock in the company and a seat on the board of directors as vice president.

The $10,000 went quickly—and when Shipman and Bowker asked Jones for the remaining funds, Jones didn't have it. His house hadn't closed, so in the interim, Bowker lent Jones the $20,000. "Here he was, our high-rolling investor," Shipman would recall years later, "and he was just a guy, just like us."

With the seed money in place, Shipman gave notice at Ste. Michelle, where it was agreed that he would stay until the end of August. His next task was to find a brewmaster. Shipman approached Joel Klein, Ste. Michelle's master winemaker, and asked if Klein could recommend a brewmaster, or at the very least, a place to look for one. Klein suggested Shipman contact Joe Dougherty—the brewmaster at Olympia Brewery and the head of the Washington State Brewmaster's Association.

A few days later, Shipman drove to Olympia and met with Dougherty. Shipman explained to Dougherty that he was going to build a microbrewery like Anchor and he was looking for a brewmaster. Dougherty recommended a man in the association named Charles McElevey.

Shipman and Bowker considered themselves extremely lucky to find a brewmaster with credentials as impressive as McElevey's. He had a top-notch resume in the brewing industry, with a degree in brewing engineering from Weihenstephan, a prestigious German brewing school affiliated with the Munich University of Technology. He also had more than eighteen years of brewing experience. McElevey, at forty-eight, was a bright, technically oriented man who had worked in all facets of the brewing industry. While studying at Weihenstephan from 1962 to 1967, McElevey worked between school vacations in breweries and malt houses in Nuremberg, Germany, as a brewer, maltster, and quality control technician. Along the way, McElevey became fluent in German. In 1967, after receiving his degree in brewing engineering from Weihenstephan, McElevey returned to the United States with his wife, Karin, and their two children, and accepted a position as assistant brewmaster at the Rainier Brewery in Seattle.

Four years later, McElevey was promoted to brewmaster, responsible for supervising two assistant brewmasters, three foremen, and a crew of about forty. McElevey was a no-nonsense man. He demanded a lot from those working for him, and if people were efficient and got their work done early, McElevey could always find more for them to do. McElevey, it was known around the brewery, didn't tolerate fools. He was bold, and if someone said something incorrect, he would point it out immediately.

Although McElevey was the junior brewmaster, he was head and shoulders above the rest of the crew in terms of brewing knowledge and education. McElevey had a five-year education in brewing and brewing engineering under his belt to the other brewmasters' six months at the Siebel Institute in Chicago. What's more, McElevey was smart and opinionated, and his junior rank and superior education sometimes created friction among the brewmasters.

McElevey, of Scottish descent, was legendary in the brewery for his sense of thrift. One day a mash filter arrived in a wooden crate. McElevey used the two-by-fours from the crate to finish off a wooden step-wall that butted up to the foundation of his house. "As luck would have it," McElevey later told a coworker, "I didn't even have to cut them."

McElevey always drove a used car. He was an avid elk hunter, and before hunting season, he would buy a vehicle like a Chevy Suburban to go hunting. At the end of the season, he would sell it. The next year, he would buy another one. Money is a lot easier to carry around than an old car, McElevey would say.

His climb up the Rainier corporate ladder was a steady slog. By 1974, he had been promoted to director of engineering, which gave him experience with budget preparations, project cost proposals, quality improvement, and expansion plans. McElevey also learned how to work with government agencies on building permits, water supply, sewage control, pollution control, and energy use.

In 1978, Rainier was purchased by G. Heileman Brewing Company, and McElevey left the company. He went to Central America, where he worked from May 1978 through 1979 as production manager for the Compania Cervecera de Nicaragua (CNN), a large brewery in Managua, Nicaragua. But the political turmoil in the country worried McElevey, so he returned to the states and started a brewing consulting practice

McElevey, a practical, frugal man, was exactly the kind of person Shipman and Bowker needed to help them start their brewery. He could design a brewery, build it, brew its beer, and then manage brewery operations.

Shipman and Bowker were elated to have found McElevey, but McElevey wasn't so sure about Shipman and Bowker. It seemed odd to him that these two marketing types wanted to build a brewery, especially since neither of them knew the first thing about making beer.

The first meeting between the three men was held at Swannies Underground, a restaurant and nightclub in Seattle's Pioneer Square. Shipman and Bowker laid out their plans for building a brewery and described the consulting arrangement they wanted him to consider.

To McElevey, it was obvious that Shipman and Bowker needed a lot of help. He had reservations about working with them, but the opportunity to build a microbrewery and brew a new beer sounded like fun, so he tentatively agreed to the arrangement.

McElevey could be an intense man, especially when working, but he also had a good sense of humor. At the end of the meeting, McElevey looked directly at Bowker and asked, "How old are you?"

"Thirty-eight," Bowker said.

Then McElevey turned to Shipman. "How old are you?"

"Twenty-eight," Shipman said.

"I don't know what the hell I'm doing with you guys," McElevey said. He was only half-joking.

Later that year, McElevey signed an employment agreement with Shipman and Bowker to serve as consultant and brewmaster for the fledgling brewery on a temporary basis from August 1, 1981, through December 1, 1983—in exchange for up to nine hundred shares of common stock and a gross salary of $2,000 a month.

CHAPTER FIVE

LOOKING FOR TELESCOPES

AFTER VISITING THE ANCHOR BREWERY, it was clear to Shipman that building a brewery was an expensive endeavor—even if they cut corners. Shipman didn't know how much Maytag had spent on Anchor, but he figured that it was more than their budget allowed. Shipman calculated that to build a brewery and stay afloat until the company became profitable, they needed $350,000. To raise the capital, he proposed that they finance the brewery with a private stock offering aimed at individuals of high net worth in the Seattle area.

Shipman, optimistic about the prospect of finding private investors, predicted that they would have to chase investors away. Bowker was much more skeptical. He knew that finding investors for a brewery would be an uphill battle. Starting a brewery in the early '80s was not the most popular of ideas, as he discovered when he shared his plan with an investment banker.

"Start a brewery?" the man croaked. "Breweries don't start up, they shut down."

His statement was supported by plenty of evidence. The history of the American brewing industry had been, by and large, a series of failures and consolidations. Breweries reached their peak in terms of the numbers in 1873, with a total of 4,131. Most of these breweries were small establishments that served the local population. But by 1910, the number dwindled to 1,568.

There were several reasons for the phenomenal drop in the number of small breweries. With the advent of the railroad, ambitious breweries such as Anheuser-Busch could expand into national markets. Industrial refrigeration, coupled with the relatively new pasteurization process, meant that bottled beer could be shipped greater distances and kept for longer periods of time. Expansion efforts were helped along by the invention of the crown bottle cap in 1892 by Thomas Painter. The new bottle cap further extended the shelf life of beer and enabled regional breweries to extend their reach to a national scale. At the same time, small breweries were hampered by a federal law, not repealed until 1910, that prohibited brewing and bottling beer on the same premises. Most small-scale brewers couldn't afford the extra expense of maintaining a separate building for bottling, so they either consolidated or went out of business. Meanwhile, breweries that *could* afford to bottle, such as Anheuser-Busch and Pabst, expanded into new territories and got richer.

Prohibition, enacted in 1920, dealt another severe blow to the industry. By the time Prohibition ended in 1933, only about half of the country's roughly 1,500 breweries resumed operation, and those that reopened faced the heightened competition brought on by the Depression. What emerged in the wake of the Depression was a centralized industry of large breweries that produced mass-market lager beers that may have been universally appealing, but were also sadly lacking in character.

By the late '70s, the two largest American brewing companies, Anheuser-Busch and Miller, accounted for more than 40 percent of the market share in the United States. By 1980, their collective market share would increase to nearly 50 percent.

In the shadow of the centralized American brewing industry, a cottage industry of craft breweries emerged in the '70s and early '80s to satisfy the sophisticated beer drinker. In addition to Anchor, a handful of small breweries sprung up on the West Coast. In California, the craft breweries included New Albion in Sonoma; DeBakker in Navotto; River City Brewery in Sacramento; and Sierra Nevada in Chico. In Portland a small brewery called Cartwright's had opened in 1979 and in the same year, the Boulder Brewing Company had opened in Boulder, Colorado. These small, independent breweries filled a market niche left untouched by the major breweries. They offered the sophisticated beer drinker a locally produced beer that was not only fresh, but full of character.

In July 1981, as Shipman worked out the details of the stock offering, Bowker and Heckler worked on a name and label for the beer. Bowker compiled a long list of names, parked himself in a coffee shop, and narrowed the choices down to a list that included the likes of Coho and Chinook, names of salmon indigenous to the Northwest. From among the names that he had written on a piece of paper, Bowker circled *Redhook.* It was immediately recognizable, it contained the letter *k,* and it bore no association to any existing product. It was also flexible enough, in Bowker's opinion, to accommodate future product extensions, such as Blackhook Porter, Blackhook Stout, or Redhook Extra.

Bowker later realized that he had subconsciously fallen into a pattern of naming companies and products with words that included the letter *k.* Upon reflection, he came to the conclusion that certain consonants like *k* were good, because when pronounced, the *k* sound cut through the air.

(The name for the company, the Independent Ale Brewery, would be short-lived and seldom used. After opening, most people associated the brewery with the beer and called it the Redhook Brewery. The company name, consequently, was soon changed to the Redhook Ale Brewery.)

To sell their idea to investors, Shipman and Bowker prepared a detailed prospectus that explained the business, the products it would produce, and the investment risks.

"Redhook Ale," Shipman wrote in the prospectus, "will be produced to fill a specific position in the marketplace which, in the opinion of management, is not presently occupied by an existing product: that of a freshly brewed, locally produced beverage that is competitive in both taste and price with the best-selling imported beers and ales."

Redhook, the prospectus stated, would be targeted at the sophisticated beer drinker. In the "Consumer Profile" section of their prospectus to investors, Shipman wrote the following paragraphs:

"The increasing sales of import beers is testimony to the existence of enthusiastic and experimental beer drinkers. A recent profile based on research by *Business Week* magazine reveals that import beer drinkers tend to be young (25 to 44 years), affluent, and managerial or professional persons.

"That analysis can be confirmed by a visit to certain leading taverns or restaurants in Seattle. Beyond these simple demographics, there are a few telling characteristics of this consumer group: first, the enthusiastic beer drinker has a highly developed sense of taste drawn from the world of food and wine. Further, this group has intense curiosity about the raw materials and the production techniques of the beer they drink. Beyond this, they see beer as an all-purpose drink appropriate to cocktail hour and mealtime. These characteristics show a consumer who is radically different from the target of the major brewers, a consumer who can be served best by a local custom brewery."

Shipman and Bowker proposed pricing Redhook at the top of the market, with a small, but distinct price advantage over certain imported beers and ales that were pioneering the high-priced keg market in Seattle. Redhook would be higher than domestic super-premium beers such as Michelob, brewed by Anheuser-Busch, Henry Weinhard's by Pabst, Erlanger by Schlitz, or Lowenbrau by Miller. But Redhook would sell for less than a keg of Guinness Stout from Ireland or Watney's from England.

A 15.5 gallon keg of Michelob Dark, for example, retailed for $33.50, while a 13.2 gallon keg of Watney's or Guinness Stout sold for $67. Redhook would be priced at $60 for a 15.5 gallon keg, the same price Fritz Maytag charged for a keg of his Anchor Steam beer.

In Seattle taverns, Watney's, Guinness, and Anchor Steam were selling for $1.75 a pint. Redhook would be similarly priced, offering tavern owners a relatively high profit per glass.

In the prospectus, Shipman pointed out several trends that made Seattle an ideal city for starting up a microbrewery. Per capita consumption of import beer was among the highest of any U. S. city. What's more, Seattle was a city that supported local products. Geographically isolated in the upper corner of the Pacific Northwest, its quirky locals supported Ste. Michelle wines, Sunny Jim Preserves, Starbucks coffee, and Rainier beer. Rainier beer, the prospectus stated, was the only major beer brand brewed in Seattle and enjoyed a 30 percent share. And locally produced Chateau Ste. Michelle wines held the highest market share for any premium wine brand in any city in the United States.

Initially, the brewery would produce only keg beer. Bottling, they proposed, would come later. The kegs would be delivered to the best taverns, bars, and restaurants in the Seattle area, where the most influential taste leaders would help to develop product loyalty. Redhook, they proposed in their prospectus, would be hard to get, encouraging local partisans to seek it out. Shipman negotiated a deal with Gary Raden, a prominent distributor of beer and wine in western Washington. The delivery truck, it was decided, would be painted with the Redhook signature, and a full-time driver-salesman would be assigned to deliver kegs to accounts. This driver-salesman, although an employee for the distributor, would be a key person in the Redhook marketing plan, and would spend extensive time at the brewery learning about the product and the brewing process in order to communicate product values to customers.

Shipman and Bowker lacked a budget large enough to create media advertising, so they decided to rely on word-of-mouth recommendations and free coverage on local television, radio, newspapers, and magazines. "Word-of-mouth support for Redhook would be encouraged by careful package positioning and through the sale of point-of-purchase material such as coasters, posters, tap-markers, and collateral materials such as T-shirts and mugs," Shipman wrote in the prospectus. "The company will actively seek to tap the reservoir of free editorial media interest in Redhook Ale. Radio, television, newspaper and magazines have an active and continuing interest in small, 'romantic,' traditional businesses in Seattle, and these opportunities will be carefully orchestrated and exploited."

In the prospectus, Shipman stated that the brewery would produce and market Redhook Ale in small batches, using high-quality materials. Redhook Ale would be a "true ale, fermented with the yeast strain *Saccharomyces cerevisiae*, a top-fermenting yeast rarely used in the United States." The ale would be brewed from malted barely and water, with the addition of hops complementary to British ale. The color of Redhook Ale would be medium—approximately 20 degrees Lovibond—a color similar to that of Anchor Steam Beer or Samuel Smith's Old Brewery Ale, two beverages well established in the marketplace. It was anticipated that Redhook Ale would have an alcohol content of 3.9 percent by weight to meet government regulations.

To house the brewery, Shipman found a four-thousand-square-foot building in Ballard that had been previously used as a transmission repair facility. The building, which was vacant, was owned by Mason Williams, a young salesman of marine lubricants who had a taste for investing in real estate in the Ballard area. The building wasn't for sale, so Williams was surprised to get a call from Shipman inquiring about its availability.

The facility was covered with transmission oil and Williams was cleaning it at the time. He had tentative plans to use the building as a storage area for his products—but when he got a call from Shipman, he agreed to meet him at the building and give him a tour.

When Williams met Shipman and walked him through the building, Shipman began taking measurements. Satisfied with the building's dimensions, Shipman told Williams that he wanted to lease the facility for five years.

"OK," Williams replied.

"But we don't have any money," Shipman said.

Williams agreed to let Redhook pay a reduced amount of rent for a two-year period, until the brewery could be established. After that, the rent would rise incrementally each year. Williams also agreed to clean the building and remove the containers of old transmission oil from the premises.

By mid-August, the prospectus for the Redhook Brewery was nearly complete. Shipman camped out at the law offices of Riddell, Williams, Ivie, Bullitt & Walkinshaw in Seattle to finalize the legal details of the stock offering. To capitalize Redhook, Shipman and Bowker had decided to raise $350,000 through the sale of common stock. They would sell the stock in blocks of 480 shares at $36.50 per share. All funds paid by investors would be placed in escrow with Rainier National Bank until the company received subscriptions for at least 4,800 shares, amounting to $175,000—the minimum required capitalization.

Shares would be offered only to individuals who represented in writing that they had a net worth (exclusive of home, home furnishings, automobiles, restricted securities, and other nonmarketable assets) in excess of $100,000, or a net worth in excess of $75,000 and an annual gross income above $50,000.

The bottom line was that Shipman and Bowker needed ten investors, each with $17,500—before January 31, 1982. If they found their investors in the allotted time, the funds would be released to the company. If they did not, the funds would be returned to subscribers with interest and the offering would be terminated.

By September 15, 1981, the prospectus was finished and approved by the lawyers and accountants, and Shipman, Bowker, and Jones were ready to commence the offering of Redhook stock. But state law called for a thirty-day waiting period before they could sell stock in the state. In the interim, Jones put together a meeting of potential investors at the Marriott Hotel in Denver, Colorado. Bowker invited a friend along to the meeting, Gordon Price, a banker from Colorado Springs.

During the meeting, Bowker and Shipman pitched the idea of investing in the brewery, but none bit—except for Price, who handed over a check for $17,520. Shipman was ecstatic. Bowker was more cautious.

"It's not going to be that easy," Bowker warned Shipman.

Bowker's words rang true. They wouldn't see another check until Thanksgiving.

Bowker believed that those who understood the prospectus realized that the investment involved a high degree of risk and did not invest. For starters, the offering involved a substantial immediate dilution from the offering price of $36.50 per share. Upon completion of the sale of all of the offered shares, the net tangible book value per share would decrease to $17.26 per share. If Shipman and Bowker were successful in selling only the 4,800 shares to meet minimum capitalization, the net tangible book value of investors' shares would be $11.28 per share.

The new brewery also ran the risk of undercapitalization. As Shipman stated in the prospectus, unless the brewery could obtain adequate financing from the sale of shares or from other sources, it would be undercapitalized and might not be able to fully equip the brewery or to profitably carry on its business. There were no assurances that the company's operations would be profitable in the future or that future revenues would exceed the company's expenses. Accordingly, an investor was undertaking the risk of losing their investment in its entirety.

The operations of the company were also subject to the general conditions existing in the beer industry, as well as the national economy. These risks included potential wage and price freezes or other restrictions imposed by government authorities, changes in federal, state, or local tax laws applicable to the company. They also included the availability of skilled labor, and availability of capital for future needs. As Shipman wrote in the prospectus: "Increases in the cost of raw materials, taxes, energy, and labor would adversely affect the financial performance of the company, unless such costs can be passed on to the consumers; and there is no assurance that prices of the Company's products can be adjusted to offset such increases in expenses."

The new company also had no diversification. Nearly all of the assets of the company would be committed to the production and sale of Redhook Ale. Since the brewery would not have other assets or product lines to spread the risk of investment, the company's profitability and the return on the investor's purchase would depend solely on the success of the sales of Redhook Ale, and there was no guarantee that Redhook Ale would be accepted in the marketplace.

Sales of the product would depend, in part, on consumers' acceptance of a trade name and logo which were unknown. Competitors, on the other hand, had well-known trade names and logos and would benefit from superior brand recognition in the marketplace. Sales of Redhook Ale would also depend on the development of consumer tastes toward a high-quality, locally produced premium ale. "There can be no assurance," Shipman wrote in the prospectus, "that this product will be well received by the consuming public."

Competition also posed a significant threat to the survival of the brewery. Shipman and Bowker were attempting to gain a foothold in a highly competitive market, and the products which the brewery would produce would be in direct competition with similar, well-established products from other companies, many of which had deep pockets for advertising campaigns. "Such competitors could at any time enter the market with a substantially equivalent product," Shipman wrote, "which may have competitive advantages over Redhook."

Of all the twenty-three potential risks that Bowker and Shipman listed in prospectus, the biggest possible risk factors were perhaps "Inexperienced Management," and "Risk of Loss of Key Personnel."

Under "Inexperienced Management," Shipman wrote that "Management has not had any specific experience in organizing or operating a brewery business. Brewery operations will be under the supervision of Mr. Charles McElevey."

Under "Risk of Loss of Key Personnel," Shipman wrote: "Management of the Company will be dependent to a large degree on the services of Charles McElevey, brewmaster. Loss of the services of Mr.

McElevey could have a material adverse effect on the business of the Company in that another qualified brewmaster may be difficult to find or impossible to retain."

In Bowker's opinion, the people who invested were emotional investors. They either liked the idea of the brewery or the product, or they were compelled by Shipman or Bowker to invest.

One of those who invested without fully reading the prospectus was Mick Schreck, a leasing agent for commercial real estate. Schreck had been referred to Bowker and Shipman by Mick McHugh—a Seattle restaurateur and friend of both Schreck and Bowker. Schreck met Bowker and Shipman at the Hunt Club in downtown Seattle.

Years later, Schreck recalled that he had no reason to read the prospectus. "All I can remember was that I was making the investment based on the fact that Bowker was a creative guy, and I was betting on his creativity. And Shipman was dripping with enthusiasm."

Another enthusiastic investor was Mark Torrance, who was referred by Peter Dow, owner of the Café Juanita on Seattle's east side. Torrance, whose start-up company Yesco pioneered popular music in restaurants, thought the idea of producing British ale was a great idea. But when he told his father-in-law about it, his father-in-law called Alan Ferguson—who had been president of Rainier during its years of decline—and asked him what he thought about an investment in beer. Ferguson told him that it was the craziest idea in the world.

People gave Shipman and Bowker all kinds of reasons for not investing. But one response that Bowker began to particularly loath was this: "No, I'm not going to invest, and I'll tell you why. Basically, I'm a lot smarter than you, and let me tell you why I'm smarter than you."

At one point, Shipman, Bowker, and a prospective investor, a high-powered marketing consultant in the beverage industry, were having lunch at Place Pigalle, a restaurant in Seattle's Pike Place Market. Just when Shipman and Bowker were ready to ask the man if he wanted to invest, he turned to Bowker and asked, "Why is it that you guys are making ales when 99 percent of the beer consumed in the United States is lager?"

"Because I say so," Bowker said, clearly incensed. His obvious wrath killed any possibility of an investment. Shipman, who managed to keep a straight face, found great humor in the incident, and years later, he would crack up laughing whenever he related the story.

At the beginning of the offering, Shipman figured they would have to chase investors away. But after they exhausted the A list, his attitude changed. By the time they'd exhausted the B list, Shipman was as nervous as a cat.

After burning through their C list, Shipman began to notice a familiar pattern. Before Bowker or Shipman could receive a check, all investors had to fill out a subscription form to certify that they met the specified financial criteria. It was embarrassing to ask them whether they were accredited and Shipman and Bowker only did it because the lawyers said they had to. But Shipman began to notice that the people who *were* accredited had telescopes in their offices. So as the deadline approached, Shipman and Bowker stopped asking people if they were accredited and started looking for people with offices that had telescopes.

Ironically, on December 31, as Shipman and Bowker scrambled to find the remaining investors to make minimum capitalization, the Multnomah County Sheriff in Portland, Oregon, padlocked the door of Cartwright's Brewery. The owner, Charles Coury, had spent more than two years producing and promoting a beer that had generated little enthusiasm in the marketplace. His goal was to make a mild ale with a low taste profile to compete with Portland's Blitz-Weinhard Beer. His equipment, however, was old and makeshift and the beer, with a high price tag of $1 per bottle, did little to encourage people to try more than one.

Cartwright's moveable equipment and the balance of the beer was auctioned off at $1 a case to pay Coury's property taxes. The feds and the landlord took the rest. Among his many mistakes, Coury had brewed the wrong beer, targeted the wrong audience, and failed to maintain quality control in the crucial early stages of the operation.

Shipman had heard about the closing of Cartwright's through his wife, who was a regulatory consultant and a former inspector for the U. S. Bureau of Alcohol, Tobacco, and Firearms. Shipman was thankful that most investors didn't know about Cartwright's failure. If the subject of Cartwright's came up in a meeting with a potential investor, he would explained that Coury hadn't paid his excise tax. "We're not like that," Shipman would explain. "We really know what's going on here."

By January 1, 1982, Shipman and Bowker were still short investors. Shipman had sold the last unit five different times. Investors promised to mail the checks, but not all the checks arrived. In the end, Shipman had to go back to the investors and get a waiver that said it was OK to extend the offering to February 28.

As Shipman and Bowker struggled to meet the new deadline, Bowker was approached by Ed Leimbacher, a producer for Heckler and Associates who was working on Rainier commercials at the time. Leimbacher knew that Shipman and Bowker were struggling to raise the money, and Bowker was a good friend of Leimbacher's, so he told Bowker he was willing to buy shares.

Both Shipman and Bowker, however, had doubts that Leimbacher was accredited.

"Look, Ed," Shipman said, "we're not going to ask you twice. Are you accredited? Are you a sophisticated investor?"

"You bet I'm a sophisticated investor," Leimbacher answered, so Shipman said "OK," checked a box on the accreditation form, and accepted the check. It can be argued that Ed Leimbacher was not the last investor, but the point is academic, because by February 28, 1982, Shipman and Bowker had met the requirements for minimum capitalization. They were now ready to start building a brewery.

CHAPTER SIX

IRRATIONAL RATIONALE

IN THE EARLY '80S, there were no small-scale manufacturers of brewing equipment in North America, so McElevey scavenged, imported, and designed his own equipment. He was a master at stretching a dollar. He got a good bid on wine tanks that would serve as fermentation vessels; he customized a milk tank to work as a cooling reservoir; he designed his own brew kettle; and he bought a used brewhouse from a brewery in Germany.

When Shipman estimated the cost of building the brewery, the minimum capitalization amount ($175,000) seemed like an ocean of cash. Once McElevey started shopping, it became clear that they were operating on a limited budget. Added to the cost of the major components—brewhouse, brew kettle, and fermentation tanks—were the incidental costs for compressors, hoses, and fittings. The brewery needed kegs and custom taps for their accounts, and McElevey would need a construction crew to help him assemble the equipment. Cleaning the transmission crud off the floor alone cost $9,000.

Cleaning the floor to brewery standards was an ordeal that spanned thirty-two days. When Shipman first inspected the building, the concrete floor was so oil soaked that he thought it was made of macadam, a type of pavement composed of small compacted stones bound with tar or asphalt.

Shipman trumpeted the epic proportions of the oil cleanup to the press. He emphasized how much money they'd spent cleaning the building because he was worried that people would think negatively of a brewery located in a transmission shop. His concerns were well founded. Chris Barnes, owner of Murphy's and Cooper's pubs in Seattle and one of the brewery's first customers, was shocked when he visited the brewery for the first time and discovered that it was located in the same building where he'd had his car worked on.

In January 1982, McElevey flew to Groeingen, West Germany, to inspect a used brewhouse that he'd seen advertised in the back of *Brauwelt,* a German brewing publication. The brewhouse belonged to the Wackerbrau Brewery, which had built a more modern plant on the other side of town. Wackerbrau was offering the brewhouse for the bargain price of 20,000 marks, equivalent to about $12,000, a fraction of what a new brewhouse would cost.

The vintage twenty-five-barrel copper brewhouse, built in 1950, featured an unusual yet efficient design. The brewing vessels were stacked on top of each other, creating a brewhouse that looked like a giant bullet. The design not only saved space, but also worked more efficiently since the bottommost vessel, the mash tun, heated the topmost vessel, the lauter tun.

To help him disassemble the brewhouse for shipping back to the states, McElevey hired a local blacksmith and mechanic. Once the brewhouse was dismantled, McElevey and his makeshift crew loaded the pieces into open-topped shipping containers that were picked up by a truck and eventually loaded onto a ship headed for Seattle. Shipping the brewhouse from Germany to Seattle cost nearly as much as the brewhouse itself.

In early March, McElevey assembled a construction crew to help him piece together the brewery components. He hired Rick Buchanan, a friend and contract plumber who lived across the street, and Bob Zahler, a friend of his daughter's.

The low ceilings of the transmission shop, combined with the stacked brewhouse design, presented some perplexing technical challenges for McElevey, so he also hired Art Hines, a retired Rainier Brewery engineer. With Hines' help, McElevey and crew set up hoists and managed to tip up the brewhouse in the transmission shop and move it into place. When it was finally upright, the topmost component of the brewhouse cleared the ceiling by only an inch.

While McElevey and his crew built the brewery and Shipman traveled the Northwest trying to raise the second half of the $350,000 called for in the prospectus, Bowker struggled to find a small-scale manufacturer of tap handles. At the time, companies that manufactured tap handles in the United States dealt exclusively with large breweries such as Anheuser-Busch and Miller. Unable to find a manufacturer who was willing to take on Redhook's order at a cost-effective price, Bowker turned to a distant relative, Regnor Reinholdtsen, for help. Reinholdtsen, a bearded Norwegian immigrant who had grown up in the same neighborhood as Bowker, was a sculptor and part-time commercial fisherman who kept a pottery studio on Sunset Hill in Ballard. Reinholdtsen had worked for Heckler and Bowker on a number of occasions, crafting various pieces for photo shoots. For an advertisement for Snowmass, for example, Heckler and Bowker had commissioned Reinholdtsen to sculpt a small rendition of the Snowmass ski resort, which was used in a Norman Rockwellesque print ad that featured a man serving Snowmass on a platter like a Thanksgiving turkey.

Bowker visited Reinholdtsen at his studio in the middle of fishing season and invited him down to the brewery for a tour. At the time, Reinholdtsen was in between fishing trips with his father. Bowker, who had attended the Great British Beer Festival in 1980, told Reinholdtsen that he wanted him to produce a clay tap handle like those he'd seen in the London pubs.

Reinholdtsen told Bowker he didn't have time to sculpt the tap handle, but agreed to look for a sculptor to take on the job. Months later, Reinholdtsen still hadn't found anyone, so he created the clay sculpture, based on drawings by Heckler, between trips. Once finished, he sent the sculpture to a mold maker in Seattle, who created a master mold and then shipped it to a small company called Del-Anne in Union Gap, a tiny town in eastern Washington, where the mold was used to create multiple ceramic tops for the tap handles.

The tap handles were hand assembled and custom made for each Redhook account. To create the tap handle, a wing nut was glued inside the sculpted portion of the tap. Then a copper pipe, which could be cut to a length specified by the customer, was screwed into the nut. When the tap handles were finished, they were visually striking, but delicate. When put into use months later, they broke with alarming regularity. Eventually, Shipman instructed bartenders not to use the tap handle like a normal tap handle. To prevent breaking the clay off from the copper, he advised, they should pull from the lower portion of the copper pipe, not the ceramic top.

Shipman, Bowker, and McElevey had originally planned to purchase a wood-clad, stainless steel brew kettle for the brewery. The cost of a new brew kettle, however, was beyond the brewery's budget, so McElevey decided to design and build his own. McElevey created two design proposals for Bowker and Shipman: one designed for using whole hops, the other designed for using hop pellets. After discussing the proposals with Bowker and Shipman, it was McElevey's understanding that the brewery was not going to use whole hops, so he built the brew kettle specifically for use with hop pellets.

After the brew kettle was built, Bowker was surprised that McElevey had designed it for hop pellets. He recalled that they had agreed to use whole hops. Bowker was insistent on using whole hops—after all, Fritz Maytag himself recommended it. In McElevey's opinion, it was too costly to change the design of the kettle, so he improvised a system with cables and stainless steel cages with doors. The cages could be filled with whole hops and then lowered into the brew kettle. When the hops had been sufficiently boiled, the cages could be reeled out of the kettle and suspended above it.

By April, McElevey was ready to begin pilot-scale brewing, an experimental phase of the brewing process that involves making small batches of beer to test the recipe and its ingredients. Based on input from Shipman and Bowker, McElevey designed a recipe for British ale that would be made in accordance with *Reinheitsgebot*, a German code of purity forbidding the use of anything other than water, malted barley, hops, and yeast. McElevey's recipe called for dechlorinated tap water, Yakima Valley hops, British ale yeast, and a blend of specialty malts and pale two-row malted barley that would give the ale a distinctive copper color.

The brewing process, whether conducted by a homebrewer or a large-scale commercial brewery, is essentially the same. Usually, malted barely supplied to the brewery is ground into griot and then immersed in water in a vessel called a *mash tun*. The water in the mash tun is then heated and kept at a controlled temperature that allows enzymes in the barley to convert starches into fermentable sugars. At this point, the beer is really nothing more than a sweet barley porridge, and the resulting aroma is the earthy, musty smell that so uniquely characterizes breweries.

After mashing, the barley porridge is pumped into a vessel known as the *lauter tun*, where the spent barley grain is separated from the liquid. The resulting liquid, known as *wort*, is then pumped into the brew kettle, where hops are added. Hops, green conelike flowers that grow on vines, have been used in beer making for hundreds of years; their bitterness provides a balance that counteracts the sweetness of the malt. Hops also inhibit spoilage and were used in the days of tall sailing ships to preserve beer on long ocean voyages. The wort is then boiled for a specific period of time—usually one to two hours—to release the resins that give beer its bittering flavor. Hops may be added several times during the boil, and different varieties of hops may be used for each addition.

After the wort has been sufficiently boiled and the hops resins have been released, the wort is pumped through a heat exchanger, which lowers its temperature to make it suitable for fermentation. The wort is then pumped to a fermentation vessel, where yeast is added to it and the fermentation process begins. Usually, after a fermentation and storage period of about three weeks, if everything goes right, the ale is ready to be consumed.

Of all the ingredients that effect the flavor of beer, the most influential and least understood is yeast—a microscopic, single-cell fungus. There are thousands of strains of yeast, and each yeast strain, whether ale or lager yeast, has a unique flavor profile. Some enhance malt characteristics, some are nutty, some are simple and clean, and some, like Belgian yeast strains, impart a unique spiciness to beer.

In the early '80s, commercial brewer's yeast could be obtained from a variety of places that maintained yeast banks, including other breweries, university microbiology labs, and microbiology labs dedicated to brewing. McElevey considered all of these options for the Redhook Ale yeast. An obvious choice would have been Schwarz Laboratories, a company in Stamford, Connecticut, that supplied not only yeast, but also microbiological consulting services to the brewing industry. But McElevey ruled out Schwarz. Their yeast was publicly available, and if he used Schwarz, he feared other breweries could get the same yeast and make a beer that would taste similar to Redhook.

McElevey knew, for example, that the Sierra Nevada Brewery was using yeast supplied by Schwarz. But McElevey was too much of a maverick to follow in the footsteps of another brewery. His charter from Shipman and Bowker had been to create a unique ale, one that gave beer drinkers a good reason for choosing Redhook over another product, and that's what McElevey intended to do.

Looking for a yeast source that was close to Seattle, McElevey called the universities in the area and discovered that the University of Washington maintained a yeast bank in its microbiology lab. McElevey contacted a professor in the microbiology department and explained that he wanted to procure some yeast strains, and that he wanted to hire a graduate student, part-time, to provide laboratory services. The professor confirmed that the microbiology department had yeast available and recommended several graduate students, one of whom was a doctoral student named Matt Hilton.

Hilton fit the bill perfectly. He was an avid homebrewer, he was a scientist who loved beer, and he maintained the yeast bank in the microbiology lab. The yeast bank was really nothing more than a small box—six inches wide by six inches long, and two and a half inches tall. Inside were little tubes of yeast strains. Hilton kept a variety of strains in the bank. Some of the strains he purchased from a brewing supply store in Berkeley, California. Other strains came from a homebrew shop on Roosevelt Avenue in Seattle. Still other strains were supplied by fellow homebrewers in the microbiology department. Homebrewing, it seemed, was not an unusual avocation for microbiologists.

For Hilton's interview, McElevey asked him to bring some samples of his homebrews. McElevey liked what he tasted. He told Hilton that he obviously had some good yeasts, so their next task would be to choose a yeast for the British ale that he was planning to brew. McElevey proposed that Hilton breed up a variety of yeast samples that they could use to conduct pilot-scale brewing experiments.

Using the University of Washington microbiology lab, Hilton grew a variety of yeast samples to a volume large enough for McElevey's use, and then turned them over to McElevey. According to McElevey, one yeast tube was labeled British ale yeast; another Samuel Smith, another Gales. Others were simply numbered.

For the pilot-scale brewing experiments, McElevey boiled up a single wort and then split the wort into four different batches. He then inoculated each batch with a different yeast. McElevey did all his experiments on beer that was less than twelve degrees Plato. (Plato is a system used in brewing to represent the potential alcohol of beer by measuring the percentage of sugar in the wort before it is fermented. Since sugar in the wort is fermented to alcohol, a higher percentage of sugar in the wort generally yields a higher percentage of alcohol.) In his experiments, McElevey was aiming for British ale with an alcohol content of just under 4 percent by weight.

By the end of April, McElevey's experimental ales were ready for tasting, so McElevey, Bowker, and Shipman got together and sampled the finished product. The beer they liked best, they decided, was the one made with the yeast marked British ale. Hilton did not particularly like the beer they selected. But who was he, Hilton thought, to question the judgment of Shipman and Bowker.

In addition to breeding the yeast into quantities large enough for fermentation, Hilton, at Bowker's behest, was asked to test the British ale yeast to ensure that it was true ale yeast. The test involved examining McElevey's ale for the presence of a chemical compound called *raffinose*, since raffinose could only be found in beer fermented with an ale yeast. Fortunately, Hilton found raffinose in the beer, proving that the British ale yeast strain was, indeed, a true ale yeast.

In early May, Bowker and Shipman began priming the Seattle press about the impending opening of their brewery. They issued a May 4 press release that read, "Redhook Ale, to be brewed at Seattle's first new brewery in more than forty years, will be available on draft in a limited number of Seattle area restaurants, taverns, and bars in July, Redhook Brewery president Paul Shipman announced today. The new ale will be brewed in the style of traditional English ales."

Although no official date had been set for the opening, Shipman and Bowker had been getting pressure for months from Mick McHugh, a Seattle restaurateur, to pick a date for the first pouring of Redhook Ale. McHugh, a longtime friend of Bowker's, had learned about the plans for a microbrewery as early as August 24, 1981, when Bowker called him and asked if he could recommend any potential investors. McHugh, a co-owner of two upscale restaurants in Seattle, always enjoyed giving his patrons a sip of something different, so when Bowker told him he was starting a microbrewery and looking for investors, McHugh became extremely excited by the prospect of a new brewery and told Bowker he was more than willing to help. McHugh, as a restaurant owner, could not legally invest in the venture, but he supplied Bowker with several names.

McHugh and Bowker's friendship went back a long way—to 1965—when they had worked together as guides for Seattle's underground tour. Their friendship endured, and years later, when McHugh became co-owner of Jake O'Shaughnessey's and F. X. McRory's restaurants, McHugh struck an agreement with Bowker and Jerry Baldwin to be Starbucks' first wholesale account.

From the moment McHugh heard about Bowker's plans for a brewery, he began dreaming up schemes for introducing Redhook Ale to Seattle. McHugh was an ebullient Irishman with a gift for public relations, and he was determined that the first pouring of Redhook Ale would be held at Jake's. After all, McHugh and his partner, Tim Firnstahl, had introduced several other premium beers to Seattle, including Guinness Stout, Henry Weinhard's, and Fritz Maytag's Anchor Steam, so it seemed only natural that they should introduce Redhook.

McHugh and Firnstahl, wunderkinds of the Seattle restaurant business, had long been champions of specialty beers. They prided themselves on serving their customers with products they normally couldn't get in the state of Washington. In McHugh's opinion, people in Seattle traveled more and read more than people in the rest of the country. And when they went to Europe and came home, Coors and Budweiser just wouldn't cut it. They were looking for something different.

When McHugh and Firnstahl opened Jake's in 1975 and McRory's in 1977, most Washington bars had two beers on tap: Olympia and Rainier. For draft beers, there was very little choice. At the time, Anchor Steam wasn't available, so McHugh and Firnstahl had decided to tie in with Charlie Finkel and his company, Merchant Du Vin, which represented an extensive line of exotic imported beers. Although McHugh and Firnstahl featured as many as three hundred different brands of bottled beers in their restaurants, they always preferred getting fresh draft beer.

After returning from a trip in Ireland, McHugh became interested in getting Guinness Stout on tap at Jake's. In his conversations with the Guinness representatives in Seattle, McHugh mentioned that he really needed a different beer glass to serve Guinness because he noticed that when he was in Dublin, Ireland, the bar patrons would say "Give me a jar of Guinness." When McHugh asked Dubliners what a jar meant, they told him that it meant a pint.

The European pint is twenty ounces, which in McHugh's opinion, represented a pretty good meal. With a twenty-ounce glass, the beer would get warm, especially by American standards, so he decided that for his restaurants, he needed to start with a U. S. pint. But when McHugh began looking through his restaurant supply catalogs for a pint beer glass, he couldn't find one.

One day, however, he was looking through the Libby Glass Catalog and on the last page, he found a mixing jar for hand stirring martinis and manhattans. Typically a bar would own about two or three mixing jars and they would keep them on the bar full of ice. McHugh wondered if he could use the mixing jar as a glass to serve beer in, so he called Libby and told them that he needed the mixing jars heat treated because he planned on washing them often. The Libby representative told McHugh that the Libby Mixing Glasses were one of their slowest selling items, and as a result, they had very few in their inventory.

"I'd like to try them as a beer glass," McHugh told the representative. "And I want six cases to try them out."

The sixteen-ounce glasses—known as a *pint glass* or a *pounder*—quickly became popular at Jake's, and eventually became widely accepted as one of the standard serving glasses for beer in Seattle, if not the entire country.

By late May, McHugh insisted that Bowker and Shipman pick a date for the introduction of Redhook. "We've got to do this right," McHugh told them. "We can't just take a keg of Redhook down to a tavern in Ballard and open it up. We need some lead time. We've got to pick a date and stick with it."

But Shipman and Bowker waffled. While intrigued with McHugh's plans, they were more concerned about how they were going to convert a transmission shop into a brewery. But McHugh was relentless.

"Listen," McHugh constantly reminded Bowker and Shipman. "I don't care what the date is. You just pick it."

By the end of May, Lynne Berry, McHugh's public relations specialist, had compiled a preliminary list of people to invite to the Redhook opening. While the list contained Seattle dignitaries and local media mavens, McHugh thought the event deserved statewide attention, so he suggested to Bowker and Shipman that they invite John Spellman, the governor of Washington.

"We've got to make this a big deal," McHugh exhorted Shipman and Bowker. They were, after all, opening a new business during down times in the state economy. Spellman, McHugh reminded them, was a great Irishman who always enjoyed a good pint and loved smoking his pipe. If they got Spellman—with his pipe and a pint and his fatherly image—to endorse the product out of the chute, McHugh figured, they would be well on their way to success.

When McHugh contacted Spellman, the governor was receptive to the invitation, but made no firm commitment to attend. A few days later, Shipman called him to stress the importance of his attendance. Shipman told Spellman that they were willing to plan the opening of Redhook around his availability. As it turned out, Spellman was scheduled to be in Seattle on Wednesday, August 11, so Shipman and Bowker agreed to hold the first pouring of Redhook on that date.

With Spellman confirmed, McHugh decided to invite Seattle mayor, Charles Royer, who often frequented Jake's bar when he worked the night beat for King TV.

"We've got the governor coming to the opening," McHugh told Royer over the phone, "and we'd love to have you too."

"I'd be honored to attend," Royer said.

"We've got two heavy hitters here," McHugh said to himself as he hung up the phone. "This is going to be great."

An Irish tenor named Robert Julien was a bartender at Jake's at the time. Julien sang behind the bar, and on off nights, sang in the chorus at the Seattle Opera House across the street.

"Listen, Robert," McHugh said to him, "we'd like you to hold forth with some songs for the opening."

Julien, of course, agreed. Several days later, McHugh got a call from Bowker, who told McHugh that he had found a group called the Mossy Back Morris Men, a faction of a traditional group that went from pub to pub in England, dancing, whacking sticks at each other, and performing for their ale. McHugh liked the idea, so the Mossy Back Morris Men were added to the lineup.

Ironically, while McHugh snowballed the August 11, high-noon introduction of Redhook Ale into the biggest media event since the rollout of the Boeing 747, McElevey and his crew were back in the old transmission shop still assembling pieces of the brewery. At that point, McElevey hadn't brewed an ounce of beer with the stacked brewhouse. Perhaps even more importantly, the custom-made fermentation tanks had yet to arrive from the manufacturer, JV Northwest.

One of the things Shipman appreciated most about Bowker was that he always had interesting insights into a particular situation. In an effort to rationalize the decision to move forward, Bowker invoked the fallacy of the scientific method, which he remembered had been pointed out by Niels Bohr, the Nobel prize-winning physicist. As Bowker interpreted the argument, any decision to move forward was essentially irrational, because to move forward meant that you stopped collecting data, which was in itself, irrational.

Shipman and Bowker used this rationale to guide them through the uncertainty of starting the business, raising the capital, and building the brewery.

"The idea was that nobody would rationally make a decision to build a brewery," Shipman later recalled, "so we were not pretending to be rational about it. The decision to pick a date was made with the acceptance that the decision would force a series of other decisions. You could always come up with a reason for opening later. But one day you had to actually open the doors."

Redhook's first brewery was located in an old transmission shop. When Chris Barnes, owner of Murphy's Pub, first visited the brewery, he was surprised to discover that it was located in the same building where he'd had his car worked on.

The Redhook Ballard Brewery in its early stages. Once the brewhouse was tipped into place, the top most component barely cleared the ceiling.

Judging by their smiling faces, this picture was taken before Redhook's grand opening on August 11, 1982, at Jake O'Shaughnessey's, when Redhook's infamous "banana beer" was introduced to Seattle. In the background is the vintage 1950 German brewhouse. Holding glasses of the original Redhook aloft are from left to right: Paul Shipman, Charlie McElevey, Mick McHugh, Tim Firnstahl, and Gordon Bowker.

Paul Shipman, Redhook president (left) and Charlie McElevey, brewmaster, posing in front of the Redhook brewhouse before the August 11, 1982, grand opening. McElevey purchased the used brewhouse in Germany for about $12,000—about what it cost to ship it back to the U. S. Shipman, twenty-nine years old, had great hopes for the fledgling brewery.

Redhook's driver Tom Milner pushes Redhook's inaugural keg into Jake O'Shaughnessey's for the grand opening. From left to right those with buttons on their lapels are Charlie McElevey, Gene Danielson, Tom Milner, and Paul Shipman. To the far right is Wally Walker, one of Redhook's original investors. Walker played basketball for the Seattle Supersonics at the time. He is now general manager of the Supersonics.

Mick McHugh lined up Washington Governor John Spellman (left) and Seattle Mayor Charles Royer (second from left) for the grand opening. After taking his first taste of Redhook, Royer smacked his lips and proclaimed: "This is no quiche eater's beer." Robert Julien, Jake's singing bartender, is standing in the background, getting ready to serve Seattleites their first tastes of Redhook.

n 1982, Redhook needed only one truck to deliver its beer, which was distributed by G. Raden nd Sons in Seattle.

In 1985, bottling in the Ballard Brewery was done mostly by hand. It was the dark ages of bottling for Redhook. Here Shane York pulls bottles of Ballard Bitter off the line and puts them in milk cartons. The number of labels needed was determined by the number of milk cartons filled. The labels were given to a receptionist who hand stamped a "bottled on" date on each label. The following day, labels were applied by hand.

.edhook's custom-made clay tap handles broke with alarming :gularity. To prevent the clay top from breaking off from the ɔpper piping, Shipman advised bartenders to pull from the bottom f the handle. The bartender in the photo is using the correct :chnique. The tops for the tap handles were designed by Terry Ieckler of Heckler and Associates, and sculpted by Regnor Rein- oldtsen, a fisherman, scultpor, and distant relative of Bowker's.

Showing off two of the winners in the Best of Seattle survey is Gordon Bowker with mugs of Red Hook beer and Starbucks coffee. In the background are the kegs and copper brew kettle of Independent Ales in Ballard, makers of Red Hook.

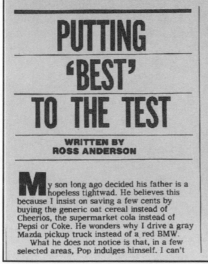

PUTTING 'BEST' TO THE TEST

WRITTEN BY ROSS ANDERSON

My son long ago decided his father is a hopeless tightwad. He believes this because I insist on saving a few cents by buying the generic oat cereal instead of Cheerios, the supermarket cola instead of Pepsi or Coke. He wonders why I drive a gray Mazda pickup truck instead of a red BMW.

What he does not notice is that, in a few selected areas, Pop indulges himself. I can't stomach canned coffee, so I buy whole coffee beans and grind them every morning. I am offended by watery, mass-market beer, and opt whenever possible for Grants Ale, Red Hook, Ballard Bitter or any of the more expensive micro-brewery ales that have proliferated in the Pacific Northwest.

Perhaps this constitutes a grave contradiction. Why save a few cents by buying the generic cereal and then immediately squander my savings on $6-per-pound coffee or $2.50-per-pint brew?

If this is supremely illogical, then I can derive some consolation from the results of the third annual "Best of Seattle" survey, which suggests that there are a few equally illogical souls out there. The Real World market, of course, is dominated by the likes of Budweiser, Folgers and McDonalds, who have bought their domination with enormous TV ad budgets. But our unscientific, self-selected pool of judges overwhelmingly opts for a few of the small, unadvertised pleasures like Starbucks coffees, Red Hook ales and Kidd Valley cheeseburgers.

Apparently there is a quality to each of these more costly items that generates loyalty — in Seattle, at least. Somehow, each of these products has managed to find a small but profitable niche at the top end of a mass

Continued on Page 12

Gordon Bowker perfected the art of boredom, and in doing so, was able to recognize two brilliant ideas when they came along: Starbucks and Redhook, both companies that he cofounded. Notice the original Starbucks logo on the coffee cup shows the entire seductive mermaid, which was later changed to make it more politically correct.

Michael Jackson, the London-based author of *The World Guide to Beer*, tasting Redhook for the first time. Jackson remarked that it tasted more like a Belgian Ale than a British Ale. Jackson's comments prompted Bowker and Shipman to change the positioning of Redhook from a British beer to a Belgian beer. Brewmaster McElevey is on Jackson's right.

The Fremont Trolley Barn served as a terminus for the Seattle Electric Railway in the 1940s. In more recent years, the building had been used to store garbage trucks for the city, and had, at one time, been a candidate for demolition. Redhook renovated the building in 1987, transforming it into one of the most technically advanced breweries in North America.

Rick Buchanan standing behind the Steinecker brewing equipment in the Fremont Brewery. With the automated brewing equipment, Redhook vastly improved the quality of its beer.

Build it and they will come," was Shipman's philosophy toward building he Fremont Brewery. When asked if Redhook was abandoning its roots as maker of hand-crafted ales in this new high-tech brewery, Shipman eplied: "You don't taste the automation, you taste the brewing."

Bartender Nelson Jay stands in front of Redhook's Trolleyman Pub. Bowker and Shipman thought that no one would ever visit the pub because of its obscure location, so they put a switchboard behind the bar so the bartender could serve as the company's receptionist. In the first full year after opening, the Trolleyman sold over $1 million of beer.

edhook's Woodinville Brewery, built in 1993-1994. Designed by architect Skip Satterwhite, a one-
man show working out of his house, the brewery is modeled after the Andechs Brewery in Germany.
hipman coined a phrase to describe the architectural style of the brewery: *Nouveau Bavarian.*

Fermentation tanks in Redhook's Woodinville Brewery, built in 1993-1994. The brewery
is capable of producing 250,000 barrels of beer a year.

From start to finish, Redhook Ale takes about three weeks to brew.

The complete line of Redhook brews. Notice the Ballard Bitter label is different from the rest. This was done intentionally to differentiate the beer from the original Redhook, which some called "banana beer." The slogan "Ya Sure, Ya Betcha" came from Bowker and was based on an old Ballard High School cheer that celebrated the Scandinavian roots of the Ballard community. To the right of Ballard Bitter is Redhook ESB, the beer that supplanted the original Redhook.

Paul Shipman (right) shows off the brewhouse in Red-hook's Woodinville Brewery to Bruce Sandison (left) vice president of wholesaler development for Anheuser-Busch. In 1994, Redhook sold 25 percent of its owner-ship to Anheuser-Busch in exchange for the Anheuser-Busch distribution network.

CHAPTER SEVEN

BANANA BEER

THE AUGUST 11 DEADLINE created a palpable tension in the Redhook brewery. Suddenly, time was compressed. Every decision became mission critical. Despite the mounting pressure, McElevey remained confident. It was early June and the fermentation tanks would arrive within a week. McElevey promised Bowker and Shipman that he would be brewing by June, and he was convinced he could keep his promise.

On June 10, the tension simmering in the brewery reached a full boil. The state of Washington passed a piece of legislation known as the Strong Beer Bill, which allowed taverns and grocery stores to sell beer that contained more than 4 percent alcohol by weight. Shipman and Bowker saw the Strong Beer Bill as a tremendous opportunity. If they produced an ale with a high percentage of alcohol—somewhere in the 6 percent range—it would help to differentiate their product from mainstream lagers, they believed.

When Shipman and Bowker broke the news to McElevey, he was adamantly opposed.

"Even if people liked the beer," he protested, "they won't be able to drink much of it. And we have to sell more than one beer per person to start out."

But Shipman and Bowker insisted that they wanted a beer that was 6 percent alcohol by weight. McElevey, realizing he wasn't going to win the argument, reluctantly agreed to rework the beer recipe to increase the alcohol content. It would be relatively simple. He would add more malted barley to the recipe and reduce the water to increase the amount of fermentable sugars in the wort. He would also boost the hops to balance the flavor.

A few days after the passage of the Strong Beer Bill, the fermentation tanks arrived from the manufacturer, JV Northwest. The tanks, in McElevey's opinion, were in rough shape, and he and his crew had to polish the insides of the tanks before installing them. By the end of June, the fermentation tanks were in place and McElevey was ready to brew the first batch of beer. As it turned out, McElevey started brewing with the newly installed equipment on July 1, missing his June target date by only one day.

Brewing the first batch of beer was a grueling process that took twenty-two hours. The plate heat exchanger, the unit responsible for cooling the wort to a temperature suitable for fermentation, leaked under pressure. As a temporary solution, McElevey built a coil and submerged it in a tank of ice water. He then pumped the wort from the brew kettle, through the coil and into the fermentation tanks. McElevey split the wort into four separate fermentation tanks, and then inoculated each batch of wort with a separate yeast that had been supplied by Hilton.

Ironically, on the same day McElevey started brewing Redhook, Bert Grant, owner of the Yakima Brewing and Malting Company, rolled out Grant's Scottish Ale to Yakima taverns. Bowker and his wife, Celia, traveled to Yakima, a small city in central Washington, for Grant's grand opening. Grant's Scottish Ale was like a classic English bitter, of moderate strength (4.5 percent alcohol), that used twice the malt, and three times the hops, of mainstream American beers. Bowker discovered that not only was Grant's beer very good, it would be arriving soon in Seattle taverns.

Bowker didn't know what Grant's opening would mean to Redhook. Having another microbrew in Seattle would legitimize the microbrew market, he thought; it would also call attention to Redhook. But Bowker worried that Grant, by being first to market—with excellent products—would capture market share in Seattle that might otherwise belong to Redhook.

Bert Grant was a formidable competitor. He had spent his adult life, and part of his teenage years, in the brewing industry. Grant started as a lab technician at Canadian Breweries at the tender age of sixteen. At the time, World War II was raging in Europe and Grant was plucked from a technical school in Toronto to fill a vacancy left by a lab technician who'd been drafted.

In his fifteen years at Canadian Breweries, Grant steadily moved up the corporate ladder, progressing from lab technician to director of bacteriology to assistant research director. Grant designed and ran a pilot brewery for Canadian Breweries for several years, creating five-gallon batches of experimental beers. He also created a design for their main brewery in Toronto, but when his design was rejected, he left the company in frustration.

After leaving Canadian Breweries, Grant built and briefly operated a pilot brewery at Stroh's in Windsor, Michigan, and then became a freelance brewing consultant, troubleshooting brewery systems and offering advice on hops and hop extracts. In 1963, Grant built a microbiology lab and pilot brewery in his basement and ran his consulting practice from his home. He also brewed his own experimental beers.

In 1967, Grant moved to Yakima, Washington, where he took a job as the general manager for the Hops Extract Corporation of America. By 1980, Grant was financially comfortable, although not rich, and content to brew his Scottish ale in five-gallon batches in his basement. At the time, Grant sat on the board of the Washington State Enological Society, an organization, which among other things, promoted wine and beer tastings. At one tasting, a woman representing Merchant Du Vin gave a lecture that rankled Grant. She criticized beers from all the big breweries, but she hadn't brought along any of these beers for a taste comparison against the products represented by Merchant Du Vin—the company that had sponsored the event.

Grant was particularly irked when she said Budweiser and Miller were made from chemicals, and that there was nothing organic in them at all. Lunacy, Grant thought; the average American beer might have one or two so-called additives, like the preservative sulfur dioxide, but the additives were used in many packaged foods.

Upset with the way the tasting was conducted, Grant told the Enological Society that he wanted to conduct a tasting himself. He held the tasting a year later, starting with Budweiser and Miller Lite. Next, he offered a few imports, and then for the grand finale, brought out his own homebrewed Scottish Ale and Imperial Stout. The reaction to his beers was overwhelmingly positive. After the tasting, three Yakima doctors approached him and offered to back him if he would start a brewery.

Grant took them up on the offer. In February 1982, Grant moved his basement brewery to a ramshackle Victorian brick-and-stone storefront, a site originally built as an opera house. He used the pilot brewery to train two brewers while he designed a better, new, high-tech brewery for his company.

For the new brewery, Grant invented an ingenious fermentation tank that allowed yeast to work at the top in ale fashion, and then be pushed to the bottom with a shot of carbon dioxide and drained, eliminating the need for tedious hand straining. He also invented his own flame-fed kettle, which he claimed extracted the wort more thoroughly. Grant, his son, and a carpenter built the brewery in four months. By May 1982, they were brewing beer with the new system, which cost Grant only $50,000 to build.

Grant took a "ready, fire, aim" approach to starting his business. While Shipman and Bowker carefully positioned the price of a keg of Redhook beer to be slightly less in cost than imports such as Watney's and Guinness Stout, Grant followed a different strategy. He simply doubled the price of a keg of Michelob. Grant never worried about prices. His goal wasn't to get rich. Grant just wanted to make good beer. Estimating that he could break even with sales of about one thousand barrels of draft a year, he purposely designed his brewery to be small. With a five-barrel plant, Grant figured, the board of directors could drink most of the product if all else failed.

A few days after Grant introduced Yakima beer drinkers to the triple-hopped tingle of his Scottish Ale, McElevey opened the taps of the Redhook fermentation tanks to examine the beer. The results were disheartening. The beer inoculated with the British ale yeast was flat and sour. Fermentation, the process through which yeast converts sugars to alcohol, carbon dioxide, and beer flavors, had not occurred. McElevey found the same results with the second tank he checked. The beer in the third tank, he discovered, had barely fermented, but the beer in the fourth tank had fermented quite nicely. Unfortunately, the beer contained a high amount of isoamyl acetate, a chemical compound that produces the aroma and flavor of ripe bananas.

"Will we have any beer for the opening?" Shipman asked McElevey.

"We'll have beer," McElevey answered, "but it may not be the beer you want."

Concerned that the product wouldn't be ready for the opening, Bowker called McHugh and told him things weren't going well at the brewery. But it was too late. McHugh and his publicist had already invited nearly one hundred people to the August 11 opening at Jake's.

"What are we going to do?" Bowker asked McHugh.

"That's your problem," McHugh told Bowker. "I'll take care of this end of it, but you guys have got to give us something. And please don't embarrass us."

After talking to McHugh, Bowker debated with Shipman and McElevey whether to postpone the opening. But McElevey assured them that he could produce a drinkable beer in time, so they decided to proceed as planned.

McElevey faced a daunting task. He had a brewery full of equipment that hadn't been tested, he had an untrained crew, and he was brewing an experimental beer. In contemplating what had gone wrong with the beer, McElevey theorized that the three yeasts, including the British ale yeast, which had performed admirably during pilot-scale brewing, were now collapsing under the high original gravity (density) of the increased alcohol in the recipe.

Considering his looming deadline and the fact that a new batch of ale would take three weeks to produce, McElevey decided that his best, and safest, option was to brew a new batch of beer using the one yeast that had been successful. Shipman and Bowker agreed, so McElevey brewed up a new batch of wort, pumped it into the fermentation tank, and then inoculated it with the yeast.

While the beer was fermenting, McElevey and his crew cleaned the remaining three fermentation tanks. After the tanks were cleaned, McElevey inspected them. He discovered each tank had a small pool of liquid at the bottom. The crew members had left the tanks dry, so McElevey tasted the liquid, and later took it to a lab to confirm that it was polypropylene glycol—the cooling solution that circulated through the jackets of the fermentation tanks.

Suddenly, the fermentation problems made sense to McElevey. The polypropylene glycol was actually leaking into the beer space. Although it was not poisonous and posed no threat to consumers, it did have the effect of inhibiting fermentation. McElevey subsequently notified JV Northwest that there was a problem with the tanks and JV Northwest hired Art Hines and his son to fix the leaks.

Several days later, McElevey opened the tap on the one usable fermentation tank that contained beer. Shipman and Bowker, standing behind him, were elated with the results. The beer had fermented. Never mind that it tasted a little weird. It had fermented, it had carbonated, and it was a beautiful copper color.

Several weeks later, the beer was ready to be kegged for the grand opening. It had an unusual flavor, but it was definitely drinkable. Shipman's confidence swelled. He knew the beer was weird, but as he would later say, "in the kingdom of the blind, the one-eyed man is king." As Shipman saw it, Redhook was the only microbrewery in

Seattle, so no matter what they made, people would accept it as microbrewery beer.

On August 11, a picture of a smiling Charles McElevey in the brewmaster's traditional white lab coat appeared on the cover of *Seattle Weekly*. Inside the paper was a multipage feature written by reporter Eric Scigliano. The article, headlined "Hail to Ale," covered the history of beer, described the virtues of ale, uncovered the seemingly subterranean microbrewery movement, and took the reader down the pioneer beer trail that was being blazed in the Pacific Northwest by the likes of Charlie Finkel, Bert Grant, and Shipman, Bowker, and McElevey.

The article was a fitting beginning for what would be a momentous day for the Redhook Brewery. A few hours later, a few minutes before noon, a van with the distinctive Redhook logo pulled up in front of Jake's. Television cameras rolled, photos were snapped, the door of the Redhook van was unlatched, and a keg of Redhook was put on ice in a wheelbarrow. Tom Milner, Redhook's recently hired driver-salesman, rolled the wheelbarrow into a room full of awaiting media as the drums rolled and the belled and beribboned Mossy Back Morris Men danced.

McHugh, speaking into a microphone to a room filled with VIPs, media minions, and hearty ale lovers, likened the unveiling of Redhook to other great Jake's moments: when the first pint of Guinness Stout from Ireland was drawn in 1976, the first Henry Weinhard's from Portland in 1980, and the first Anchor Steam from San Francisco in 1981.

"Nothing has given me as great a pleasure," McHugh enthused, "as bringing in this product from Ballard."

When it was time to draw the inaugural pints for the governor, John Spellman, and the mayor, Charles Royer, Jake's bartender, Robert Julien, did the honors. The crowd, wondering what the reaction would be, nervously watched the proceedings. Julien passed the first pint to Spellman, who held it up to the light, smiling appreciatively at the ale's copper color. Royer received his Redhook next, and was about to take a taste, when Spellman held up his glass and proposed "a toast to Redhook, Seattle, the state of Washington, and all its people."

Royer, not to be outdone, launched into a speech about the virtues of a new Seattle business offering jobs in tough times. But Royer was only a few words into his speech when he took a sip of Redhook, stopped in his tracks, smacked his lips, and blurted, "This is no quiche eater's beer."

Royer set the tone for the evening. Everyone tried to be polite, but there was an audible murmur throughout the crowd. Everyone, it seemed, was asking the same question: "Do you taste something funny? Like bananas?"

Vince Cottone sat at one of the tables. He was head of the Brews Brothers, a group of Seattle-based homebrewers who called themselves an exceptionally pious local order of barley-venerating, hop-headed, homebrewing friars. As the Brews Brothers sat around the table staring into their half-gulped pints of Redhook, they were having difficulty reaching a consensus, until Brother Mark quaffed a mouthful and proclaimed, "Wait a minute, this stuff has an off flavor. It tastes like bananas."

"Why don't you tell Paul that?" Cottone asked.

Cottone and Brother Mark hailed Shipman to the table and told him what they thought of his beer. Shipman thanked them for their comments and walked away.

Cottone and the Brews Brothers were not the only beer aficionados who were disappointed in the taste of Redhook. Patrice Demombynes, owner of the Virginia Inn, a tavern in Seattle's Belltown neighborhood, was originally excited when he'd heard about the introduction of Redhook. Demombynes, along with his partner, Jim Fotheringham, were exwaiters who'd purchased the Virginia Inn in 1981 and slowly started changing its clientele from fishermen and merchant marines to a more diverse, progressive crowd of artists and young professionals.

At the time, the Virginia Inn was one of the few places in Seattle that had Guinness, Bass, and Beck's on tap—alongside Rainier.

They'd put Grant's Scottish Ale on tap right away and were carrying it when Redhook opened. Demombynes and Fotheringham welcomed the idea of true ales being made in the Northwest. Demombynes had heard all the ballyhoo about Redhook, and he looked forward to carrying it in his tavern.

But Demombynes, who had gone to the opening with high hopes, left completely demoralized by the ale's off flavor. Unlike many Seattleites, Demombynes knew what ale was supposed to taste like; and the ales he knew didn't taste anything like Redhook.

The undercurrent of dissatisfaction with Redhook at the opening, with the exception of the Brews Brothers' comments, was lost on Shipman and Bowker. It was also lost on Robert Julien, who was pouring the beer at Jake's, and pouring it in huge quantities. After the opening, Jake's opened the doors to the public at five o'clock. They went through a keg and a half of Redhook without ever turning off the tap.

From Julien's perspective, Redhook was more than well received by the Seattle beer-drinking public—but not without a few creative adjustments. To compensate for the lack of carbonation in the beer, Julien poured Redhook through the Guinness tap, which featured three pinholes that increased the pressure on the beer as it came through the tap, thus creating a frothier head. Without the Guinness tap, according to Julien, Redhook would never have had a head on it. By the end of the evening, ten kegs of Redhook had been consumed, setting a new Jake's record for beer sold in one day.

The opening, despite the off taste of the product, was a tremendous success. It was featured that night on Seattle TV and radio stations, and the following morning headlines about Redhook streamed across the top of Seattle newspapers. The Seattle *Post-Intelligencer* ran the headline "Redhook brews up hearty applause," and featured a picture of a smiling Spellman and Royer holding up the pints in anticipation.

In the Bellevue *Journal American*, John Marshall wrote, "The object of all this attention was Redhook Ale, which was being unveiled with copious quantities of hype and hoopla that few new products could command. It made no difference that the brewery was tiny, its production minuscule, its distribution now limited to the draft taps of a privileged few establishments.

"What matters far more in such troubled economic times," Marshall continued, "was that a group of classy entrepreneurs with big-buck backing—including Seattle SuperSonic Wally Walker—were putting out a world-class product, right here in Seattle, and the recession be damned! Besides, it was a product particularly well suited for such tough times."

In a *Post-Intelligencer* article, reporter Pamela S. Leven wrote, "Robert Julien, Jake's bartender and balladeer, declared the local product to be excellent. He said it compared favorably to traditional German and English ales when they are served close to their breweries—before they are imported and lose their freshness in 'the trip through the Panama Canal.'"

With the all the attention from the Seattle media, Redhook didn't need an advertising budget. People flocked to Seattle taverns to get their first taste of the city's gutsy new ale. At Murphy's Pub in Seattle's Wallingford neighborhood, owner Chris Barnes saw a dramatic increase in customers after he introduced Redhook. The first keg of Redhook went fast at Murphy's, selling out the first night; they went through two more by week's end. But by then, Barnes knew something was up. He was beginning to hear whispers from his customers. They were wondering if Redhook was really supposed to taste the way it did.

At Jake's, it was the same story. A few days after the opening, one of the waitresses approached McHugh and whispered, "Mick, we can't sell this Redhook, nobody likes it."

McHugh immediately got on the phone.

"We've got a problem," he told Bowker. "Nobody is drinking Redhook, and my servers won't sell it."

"Oh, God," Bowker said.

"Well, let's just get rid of what we got," McHugh replied. "But you guys have got to redo the recipe."

CHAPTER EIGHT

HOUSE CHARACTER

In September 1982, Jerry Jones, Redhook's vice president, was traveling in Seattle on business and stopped into F. X. McRory's to try a Redhook. Jones had sampled Redhook before the opening, but had never actually tasted the ale that was being served to customers.

When Jones ordered a pint, the waitress bent down and whispered in his ear: "You don't want that shit, do you? It's not very good."

Jones insisted that he did, but when he tasted it, he was inclined to agree with the waitress. The beer was overly sweet, had a lingering clove taste, smelled like bananas, and had no head on it. Jones' first thought was that he had made a bad investment. He never finished the beer. Instead, he called Bowker.

"Something's wrong with this goddamn stuff," Jones said. "Fix it."

But Bowker argued that the product had to be unique to differentiate itself in the marketplace. It wasn't an import or a domestic lager, he argued, and it shouldn't taste like one.

Redhook was unique, all right, Jones thought—uniquely awful. As Jones hung up the phone, he had the sinking feeling that Redhook's money would run out before the beer took off. In his opinion, it was taking an eternity to get Redhook out into the market.

At the time, only about twenty Seattle taverns were pouring Redhook, and selling Redhook to new accounts proved difficult, particularly with the beer's peculiar flavor.

Feedback from customers was frightening. Shipman was scared to answer the phone. One day in early September, just a month after Redhook's first pour, he got a call from Tim Firnstahl, Mick McHugh's partner, who insisted that Shipman come to F. X. McRory's immediately. When Shipman arrived at McRory's, Firnstahl was sitting at a table in front of a half-empty pint of Redhook. McHugh stood nervously behind Firnstahl.

"This is the way all these beers come back," Firnstahl said, pointing to the pint of Redhook, while McHugh stared up at the ceiling in embarrassment. "No one ever finishes them," Firnstahl continued. "This beer is a problem."

Shipman shrugged. "We're working on it," he said. "You've got to work with us on this."

Later in the day, Shipman met with Bowker and McElevey at the brewery. "We've got a problem," Shipman said. "This ale is not a commercial product."

But Bowker was extremely rigid when it came to product differentiation and marketing issues.

"We have to take a stand," Bowker said. "We're not here to make a product that appeals to everyone."

"That's true," Shipman countered, "but it's got to appeal to someone."

McElevey posited that the beer's off flavor, particularly the banana ester, was coming from the yeast. The problem might be solved by switching to a different yeast, he said. Bowker and Shipman agreed it was worth a try.

After running several experiments, McElevey decided on a yeast he'd used earlier in pilot-scale brewing experiments. At the time, it had shown signs of limited fermentation—but now that the fermentation tanks no longer leaked glycol, the yeast proved superior.

But while McElevey tested the new yeast, the criticism of Redhook Ale reached a critical mass. In the October 6 issue of *Seattle Weekly*, reporter Eric Scigliano, who so brilliantly heralded the birth of Redhook and the microbrewery movement, wrote a follow-up story with the headline "Real beer revisited."

Scigliano wrote, "Shipman admits that he's gotten complaints about Redhook's one marked deficiency—or rather, excess of sugar. Early batches of the new brew have been sweet enough to make cavities sing, with a cloying aroma that's prompted local sippers to dub it 'banana beer.'"

In the same article, Scigliano touted the virtues of a competitor. "Grant's Scottish Ale, meanwhile, suffers from no such sugariness; it's a dry, highly 'hopped' bitter, which may shock some local taste buds."

At Seattle's Virginia Inn, Patrice Demombynes and Jim Fotheringham were ready to remove the Redhook tap after the first month. Redhook Ale had become an object of derision at the Virginia Inn, and Demombynes and Fotheringham were embarrassed to serve it. Fotheringham thought that Redhook Ale tasted like Wrigley's Juicy Fruit gum. His customers held similar opinions. Some called it pineapple beer. Others called it grapefruit beer or ice tea beer.

Unless asked, the Virginia Inn never offered customers a taste of Redhook before they served it. If someone sat down and ordered a Redhook, Demombynes and Fotheringham figured the customer knew what he was doing, so they would serve the person a pint without explanation. If someone ordered a Redhook and didn't like it, Demombynes and Fotheringham would take it back and give the customer a new beer at no charge.

Unfortunately, 75 percent of those who tasted Redhook didn't like it. Some people would drink it, suffer through it silently, and then order something else. Others would take a taste and say, "This is really weird," to which Demombynes and Fotheringham would invariably answer, "Yeah, well, can I get you something else?" Serving a Redhook usually required two trips—one to take it to the customer, and one to take it back. Demombynes and Fotheringham were not only wasting time serving Redhook, they were also dumping a good portion of it, along with their profits, down the drain.

In the fledgling days of the Redhook Brewery, close personal attention to each account was a Redhook trademark. Shipman and McElevey visited the Redhook accounts on a regular basis. Shipman once boasted to Regnor Reinholdtsen, Redhook's tap handle sculptor, that he not only knew the name of every bartender that served Redhook, but the name of every customer who drank it.

During one of Shipman's regular visits to the Virginia Inn, Demombynes and Fotheringham quizzed him about what was causing the off notes in the beer. Shipman told them that Redhook was using a wild yeast that was expressive of the Pacific Northwest. They used this yeast, rather than British ale yeast, he explained, because they wanted to brew a beer that was unique and regional.

Demombynes and Fotheringham were skeptical. It was true that Redhook was unique to the Northwest (and everywhere else, for that matter), but what difference did that make if people didn't like it? Grant's, which was also on tap at the Virginia Inn, was outselling Redhook four to one. And pints of Grant's weren't being sent back and poured down the drain. Only a few months after introducing Redhook at the Virginia Inn, Demombynes and Fotheringham gave up on it, and removed the Redhook tap from their system.

One night McElevey sat at the Sloop Tavern in Ballard and watched a young man order a Redhook. The man drank the Redhook as he played a game of pool. He seemed to enjoy the beer, but when he went back to the bar for a second beer, he ordered a Rainier. McElevey approached the young man who had returned to the pool table and asked why he'd switched beers. "Don't you like the Redhook?" McElevey asked.

The young man said he loved Redhook, but he wanted to stay at the bar for a while and have some fun. Redhook, he explained, was not the kind of beer he could drink all night. That was all McElevey needed to hear. He started slowly reducing the beer's strength from

14 degrees Plato (an alcohol content of 6.25 percent) to a target of 12.6 to 12.8 degrees Plato (an alcohol content of 4.3 percent).

Brad Joseph, who tended bar at the Ballard Firehouse, believed that a pint of Redhook—with a higher alcohol content, was a good deal. But few customers at the bar shared his opinion. The Ballard Firehouse, at the time, was a blue-collar tavern that was frequented by fishermen, machinists from the Ballard shipyards, state workers, a contingent of Swedish and Norwegian retirees, and a small crowd of young adults who'd grown up in Ballard. In Joseph's opinion, his patrons were "a hard-alcohol-drinking crowd."

Joseph had never heard of Redhook until he arrived for work one day and saw the distinctive yellow tap with the Redhook logo. To entice customers to drink the fruity brew, he was instructed to give away a four-ounce sample. After tasting it, the average customer would say something like, "That's good; I guess I'll have a screwdriver."

Customers thought Redhook was a joke—especially the old Norwegian men who weren't willing to pay more than two bucks for a shot. But the Ballard Firehouse kept Redhook on tap for several good reasons: Redhook was getting publicity in the newspapers, a new, younger crowd was showing up to drink it, and it was tasting better as McElevey tinkered with the recipe.

No one could deny that in the fall of 1982, the taste of Redhook improved. McElevey switched the yeast, producing a beer that had a variety of complex flavors. The new Redhook was fruity and spicy with a noticeably clovelike flavor. Bowker tasted black pepper and cardamom. The beer still had a banana aroma, but this time it was much less pronounced.

By early November, Redhook began shipping the new beer to its accounts. McHugh, meanwhile, developed a strategy to bring his customers back to Redhook for the second go-round. To introduce his customers to the new and improved taste of Redhook, McHugh sold five-ounce tasters, as he called them, for $.50.

A strange thing happened at Jake's—and most other Redhook accounts, for that matter. Redhook developed a small but staunchly loyal cadre of drinkers. The Redhook lovers were there every night at Jake's, living the development of the beer right along with McHugh, Firnstahl, and the Redhook crew.

The Redhook loyalists not only liked the beer, they liked the story. McHugh kept customers informed of Redhook's latest changes, letting them know when they'd changed the yeast, adjusted the amount of hops, or reduced the sweetness of the beer. The loyalists at Jake's served as Redhook's testing ground, and speculating what the next pint would taste like became one of their pastimes. After each adjustment in the beer, McHugh collected feedback, and forwarded it to Bowker.

In November, just after McElevey changed the Redhook yeast, a beer-tasting event was set up for Redhook Ale and Grant's Scottish Ale at the Hall Street Bar and Grill in Beaverton, Oregon, a suburb of Portland. For the tasting, Restaurants Unlimited, which was sponsoring the event, hired Michael Jackson, the famous beer writer, as the in-house expert. Shipman, Bowker, McElevey, and Grant all traveled to Oregon for the event.

After taking a taste of Redhook, Jackson, who'd gained respect among brewers for his even-handed judgment of beers, asked Bowker the same question he always asked: "What kind of beer were you shooting for here, Gordon?"

Jackson's question was part of a technique he had developed in his early years of beer research. Uninformed criticism was one of his pet peeves, particularly when someone wrote off a good beer as tasting "funny" without taking the time to find out that they were drinking, for instance, a Berlin wheat beer that was *supposed* to taste sharp and acidic.

"We were trying for a distinctive British pale ale," Bowker said. "What do you think? How close did we hit it?"

"Well, geez," replied Jackson, who had a famously broad mind about beer flavors. "It tastes more Belgian to me."

Jackson, the first person to educate the public about beer styles, had recently spent time in Belgium, researching Belgian beers and brewing techniques. In an effort to understand the mysteries of Belgian brewing, Jackson, at one point, sequestered himself in a Belgian monastery. Through his travels, Jackson sampled a wide assortment of idiosyncratic Belgian beers, so when he tasted Redhook, he wasn't nearly as shocked by the taste as the average beer drinker was.

Bowker and Shipman jumped on Jackson's Belgian description of Redhook. A few days after the tasting, they held a meeting in Shipman's car. The brewery did not have offices, since Shipman didn't believe in them, so it was common practice for Bowker and Shipman to take a drive while they discussed sensitive issues. Shipman drove into Ballard, then looped back and headed toward Seattle down Elliot Avenue, and then circled back to the brewery. During the car ride, Bowker and Shipman decided to reposition Redhook as a Belgian ale.

The beer would stay the same, but the way it was presented, both verbally and in marketing materials, was changed to reflect the new Belgian spin. Brochures, coasters, labels, and table tents that read, "Redhook uses traditional English ale yeast, the top-fermenting *Saccharomyces cerevisiae*"were changed to read, "An ale in the Belgian style is rare in the United States. Redhook is one of the few we know: only hops, barely malt, water, and yeast are used in the hand-brewed process. It is the top-fermenting ale yeast that gives Redhook Ale its distinctive character: complex, rich with the nuances of spices, herbs, and fruits." Shipman and Bowker also visited Redhook's accounts and educated tavern owners about the new way to describe Redhook Ale to patrons.

Unfortunately, Redhook's new product positioning had almost no effect. Those who liked Redhook kept on drinking it; those who disliked it still avoided it like the plague.

Chris Barnes, owner of Murphy's Pub, had a typical reaction to the new Belgian positioning: he was suspicious, but he was willing to go along with it. Barnes, from the start, had been a staunch fan of Redhook and the microbrewery movement. At the time, Grant's and

Redhook weren't available in bottles, so microbrews brought customers into his pub.

Barnes did his best to sell Redhook. He let customers sample it first in a paper cup, and he developed a spiel to prepare customers for Redhook's unusual flavor. He assured them that what they were tasting was an intended flavor—an expression of the wild yeast that Redhook was using to produce its spicy Belgian ale.

Redhook sold well in Murphy's, which is why Barnes was willing to put up with its unique and often inconsistent flavor. Inconsistency, it seemed, was a Redhook hallmark. Some days Redhook tasted overly sweet. Other days it tasted sour. Sometimes Barnes wasn't sure if what he was tasting was intentional. There were days the kegs would spout even though they were still half full. Barnes was reluctant to return beer that he had bought, but Redhook was always gracious about taking it back, which happened on more than one occasion.

Redhook, with its spicy, fruity flavor, polarized beer drinkers. Its yeast expressed a noticeable amount of vinyl guiacol, a phenolic compound that gave the beer a clovelike flavor. Those who disliked the taste of cloves hated Redhook; those who liked it loved Redhook. The problem was, not enough people loved it. In a typical Redhook account, only about 10 to 15 percent of the customers were loyal Redhook drinkers.

Fortunately, one of Redhook's biggest fans was Michael Jackson, who had given Redhook a "Four Stars–Highly Distinctive" rating—an honor shared by only four other beers in the United States. In the March 2, 1983, edition of *Seattle Weekly*, Jackson wrote an article headlined "Hail to Western Ale," singing the praises of this unique ale.

As Jackson wrote in the article, "More than any of its contemporaries, Redhook displays that fruitiness that is a definitive ale characteristic. When this characterful ale was launched, its assertiveness came as a shock to some drinkers, which is a testimony to the blandness that has come to pass for beer. As Redhook has evolved, it has gained in hop character, not so much in bitterness as in dryness, to balance its malty body, and has become a very complex ale. Such a distinctive brew should be a matter of civic pride, and will be as the difference between beer styles comes to be better understood (just as the distinction between varietal wines already is)."

With Jackson's stamp of approval, Redhook became the preeminent producer of Belgian ale in America. But many homebrewers in the Seattle area scoffed at the idea that Redhook was a Belgian-style ale. As far as Redhook was concerned, they considered *Belgian* a euphemism for *defective*.

There actually was, however, a Belgian brewing tradition that supported the complexity and mystery of Redhook. Of all the world's great beer-producing regions, Belgium featured the most idiosyncratic beer styles. Belgium was home to bizarre and sometimes ancient brewing techniques—and many breweries claimed their own unique style, using wild yeast or bacterial cultures to produce exotic beer flavors.

By early 1983, there were rumors circulating through the Seattle homebrewing community that the Redhook yeast was infected. Paul Bulson, the manager of the Mark Tobey Pub in Pioneer Square, was among those who suspected an infection. While studying environmental engineering as a graduate student at Washington State University, Bulson had managed the microbiology lab and had been in charge of purifying yeast strains for Rainier. Bulson had also brewed his own beer using the Rainier yeast he kept in the lab. Through his brewing experiences, Bulson had become familiar with the causes of off flavors in beer, and in his opinion, there was a citrusy flavor in Redhook that was symptomatic of an infection in the yeast.

Redhook tasted terrible to Bulson, but that didn't keep him from carrying it in the pub. Bulson was an enthusiastic supporter of the microbrewery movement. He'd studied microbiology at University of Surrey in England from 1977 through 1979 and had worked in the school pub during the peak of the Campaign for Real Ale (CAMRA) movement. As a result, he had fond memories of the heavily hopped English ales and quickly became a champion for the two new microbrews—Grant's and Redhook—that had come on line at the Mark Tobey. The Mark Tobey would go through two or three kegs of Redhook a week. But for every two or three kegs of Redhook, the Mark Tobey would go through ten kegs of Grant's Scottish Ale.

Redhook and Grant's were not only fresh and flavorful, they were also highly profitable. For Seattle pubs like the Mark Tobey, microbrews brought an immediate price increase for all beer. Grant's and Redhook sold for $2 to $2.25 a pint. To maintain the perception of comparative value, local lagers such as Rainier and Henry Weinhard's, which were previously $.75 cents and $1, were bumped up to $1.75. The profit margin, especially on Henry's, was tremendous, and the customers at the Mark Tobey never batted an eye.

Bulson always suspected that Shipman knew something was wrong with his beer. But Shipman, the optimist, was the consummate marketing guy. Bulson had to give him credit. Maybe he didn't like the beer, but he stuck with it, and sold it down everyone's throat. And people bought it. Bulson had customers who wouldn't drink *anything* but Redhook.

Shipman staunchly defended Redhook as a fabulous Belgian ale when dealing with clients, but inwardly, the constant comments about Redhook's weird taste caused him tension, anger, and embarrassment. He had given up his promising career at Ste. Michelle for this Redhook adventure, but now his future seemed tenuously tied to a mysterious strain of yeast and a largely misunderstood beer.

As a result, in early 1983, a debate developed at the brewery about whether to change the yeast—again. Shipman, who maintained that Redhook was not a commercial product, wanted to try something new. He believed the company's future was linked to one thing: yeast. But Bowker insisted that Redhook had to adhere to a highly differentiated standard.

McElevey was also solidly behind the product. He'd been directed to make a beer that was unique and different, he told Shipman, and that's what he had done. Shipman eventually deferred to Bowker. He trusted Bowker's instincts, and Bowker trusted McElevey's.

One day, McElevey got a call from Eric Scigliano, the reporter who covered Redhook for *Seattle Weekly.* When Scigliano quizzed McElevey about the Redhook yeast, McElevey became incensed. For McElevey, the Redhook yeast had become a sensitive topic. He'd been getting criticism about it from a number of sources, and he believed that those who were criticizing him had no idea what they were talking about.

Several things irked McElevey about the criticism. First, it was extremely hard to get a clean yeast sample. If his critics obtained their samples from the beer, there was a good chance that they had picked up bacteria or other yeast strains from the tap line. Second, his critics claimed to have looked at the yeast under a microscope, and it wasn't possible to identify a particular yeast strain by examining it under the microscope. A series of tests were required.

McElevey characterized the Redhook yeast as a Belgian-style yeast. Under the microscope, it looked like lemon drops or sausage chains, which was different from the normal golf-ball shape of typical brewer's yeast. McElevey was certain that the yeast was a strain of *Saccharomyces cerevisiae,* but it was a unique strain that expressed itself with a spicy clove flavor characteristic of some Belgian style beers or a German Weissbier.

McElevey believed that defining a yeast strain as wild was a matter of interpretation. A wild yeast, in his opinion, was a yeast strain, otherwise known as a contaminant, that was not intended to be in the beer. Thus, if you took a wild yeast, and intentionally put it in the beer, then the yeast was no longer wild.

Some, however, claimed that Redhook had multiple strains of yeast in their beer. In 1983, Mike Hale, who would later develop Hale's Ales, had just returned from England and set up a pilot brewery in his home in Colville, Washington. Hale took a culture of the Redhook yeast and found three wild strains of yeast in it. For Hale, that explained Redhook's unusual taste. Redhook was not like any of the beers he enjoyed while in England. In his opinion, Redhook was an esoteric, odd kind of beer with an interesting house character, which resulted from the wild strains of yeast.

Redhook, he also discovered, was made to a very high alcohol standard, so there were a ton of fermentables in the beer, not nearly all of which fermented. The result was residual sweetness in the beer. For Hale, Redhook was best characterized by an old saying in the brewery industry: if a brewery makes an off-tasting product and continues to make it, it's not considered defective, it's considered house character. Redhook, it was clear, had a ton of house character.

Several months after building the pilot-scale brewery in his home basement, Hale got some friends interested and managed to scrounge up about $20,000. He used the money to buy old dairy tanks and set up his own brewery, a one-man operation called Hale's Ales, in a block building in Colville, Washington.

A year later, Hale would be followed by four new microbreweries in the Pacific Northwest: Thomas Kemper opened on Bainbridge Island, Washington, followed by the Hart Brewing Company in Kalama, Washington, and Bridgeport Brewery and Widmer Brothers in Portland, Oregon.

Many a theory was posited as to why microbreweries were springing up in the Northwest. Many would attribute it to the rainy, overcast weather that was conducive to sitting inside a warm pub sipping ale. Others would attribute it to the Northwest's diversity of taste and cultures. Shipman believed otherwise.

"We inspired people to become microbrewers," Shipman would say, years later, "because every home brewer who tasted our beer thought they could make better beer in their bathtub. They were thinking that if Redhook could be this successful with a beer that tasted this odd, just think what they could do with a good-tasting beer."

CHAPTER NINE

YA SURE, YA BETCHA

McElevey's relationship with Bowker and Shipman was cordial, but never ideal. Sometimes McElevey, who'd spent most of his adult life in the beer business, was dumbfounded by the decisions they made. One day in the spring of 1983, Shipman and Bowker asked him to brew a porter for the summer. The porter, as it was envisioned by Shipman and Bowker, would be ebony in color and formulated according to a classic London recipe that called for the use of dark-roasted malt and dark barley.

"We should be bringing out a lighter beer in the summer, not the porter," McElevey argued. "The porter is a winter beer."

But Shipman and Bowker insisted, so once again, McElevey complied.

On July 18, Redhook introduced Blackhook Porter at F. X. McRory's, and it quickly developed a small but loyal following in Seattle. Blackhook, the only draft porter brewed in the western United States, was well received by most Redhook accounts—particularly at the Virginia Inn. Owners Fotheringham and Demombynes were impressed by its taste, and put it on tap. Fotheringham thought Redhook had a good feel for what a porter should be. It tasted clean with some roasted, coffeelike flavors, and it was popular with his customers.

Blackhook was considered by most to be an improvement over Redhook. The roasted malt and dark barley mitigated the quirky yeast. But the audience of dark beer drinkers was small, so Blackhook promised an even more limited following than Redhook. The Seattle press didn't help matters either. They accused Blackhook of being a darker version of Redhook.

Several days after the introduction of Blackhook, McElevey began conducting experiments on a pale ale using the Redhook yeast. The results were disappointing. Neither Shipman, Bowker, nor McElevey were impressed with its taste. McElevey suggested conducting an experiment using the British ale yeast supplied by Hilton. But Shipman was vehement about ordering yeast from Schwarz Laboratories. The last two yeasts that McElevey had secured from the University of Washington microbiology lab hadn't worked out, he figured, so this time he wanted nothing left to chance. Sierra Nevada was using yeast from Schwarz, Shipman reasoned, so Schwarz seemed like a safe bet.

McElevey cautioned Shipman and Bowker that comingling different yeasts in a brewery could cause cross-contamination. That was the reason, he explained, why large breweries, which brewed beer with a lager yeast, chose not to brew ale with an ale yeast.

But at Shipman's insistence, McElevey ordered several different yeast strains from Schwarz Laboratories. After the yeast arrived, McElevey set up a fermentation experiment with the Schwarz yeasts and the British ale yeast supplied by Hilton. On August 17, Shipman, Bowker, and McElevey sampled the various beers and selected the one made with what McElevey called the #A sample. This beer, as it turned out, was made with the Schwarz Laboratories #96 yeast—the same yeast used by the Sierra Nevada Brewery in California.

McElevey's biggest struggle in creating the new pale ale was gauging the correct level of hops in the beer. During the brewing expirements, the bitterness of the hops was not coming through, so Shipman told McElevey to add a pound of hops per batch to the cage. At one point, the makeshift hop cages were so densely packed that Gene Danielson, the assistant brewmaster, reported to McElevey that the spent hops in the middle of the cage were dry. As it turned out, the hops had swelled in the wort, and they had become so densely packed in the cage that the wort had not been able to circulate through the hops.

Redhook broke even for the first time in July and August 1983, but for the overall year, Shipman predicted a loss. Jerry Jones, who was anxious to drum up more business for Redhook, approached a wholesaler named Murray Distributing to sell Redhook in Colorado.

Murray, considered to be the best distributor in Colorado, agreed to distribute Redhook and developed a unique strategy for introducing the beer to Denver: he would approach the city's ten best accounts, but instead of trying to sell them on Redhook, he would let the accounts pitch him on why they should be one of the first places in Denver to have it.

In September, McElevey flew to Denver for the introduction of Redhook and Blackhook. Jones met him in Denver and took him to meet Murray. Judging by the size of Murray's warehouse, it was clear that Murray dealt in high volumes. McElevey warned Murray not to order too much beer. He told Murray he expected a high level of tasting the first week or two, and then the sales would drop down to a normal level.

After talking to Murray, McElevey called Shipman in Seattle and described what he had seen at Murray's warehouse. McElevey warned Shipman not to send too much beer until a sustainable level of sales could be determined.

The September introduction of Redhook in Denver was a near repeat of the Seattle introduction. Because of Redhook's association with Jones and Murray, the excitement for Redhook in Denver was feverish. People came out to taste the beer, and the following day, the event was covered in the Denver newspapers.

After the introduction, McElevey continued from Denver to the Dominican Republic on a consulting trip. Meanwhile, Danielson and the Redhook crew—for the remainder of September and into October—worked feverishly to brew an adequate supply of beer for the Seattle and Denver markets.

In October, McElevey returned to work and tasted the beer. Both Redhook and Blackhook were infected with lactic acid. Danielson, who was running the brewery in McElevey's absence, hadn't tasted it. McElevey advised Danielson to report the infection to Shipman, but he didn't. A few days later, while McElevey was away from the brewery on a hunting trip, the infected beer was shipped to Denver.

When McElevey returned to Redhook on October 18, he discovered a tank of Blackhook was infected and sour. McElevey and his crew spent the next month on an intensive cleanup effort at the brewery. They cut wort lines to make them more accessible for cleaning and inspection, and they cleaned all the equipment twice and brushed the interiors of the hoses with a rope brush.

As it turned out, most of the infected beer that was sent to Denver was eventually returned to Redhook, so McElevey instituted an aggressive brewing schedule to make up for the shortage.

Shipman, worried about Redhook's financial losses, talked with McElevey about paying him as a consultant, rather than brewmaster, when his contract ended. He also discussed the possibility of reducing the staff, and at the end of October, he laid off Danielson and Nancy Siegal, Redhook's office manager.

For McElevey, the sour beer fiasco marked a turning point in his relationship with Shipman. There had always been an underlying tension in their relationship, but after the beer was returned from Denver, the rift between the two men widened. Those who worked in the brewery observed that Shipman and McElevey were like oil and water. They couldn't be in the same room together.

Underlying the tension was the central issue of control. Shipman wanted to be fully in charge of the brewery, and McElevey resented Shipman's intrusion into his technical domain. In McElevey's opinion, he was supposed to be in charge of brewing and Shipman was supposed to be in charge of marketing, but Shipman was constantly sticking his nose into the brewing side of the business.

Shipman was asserting his authority over all aspects of the brewery for a good reason: Redhook was losing money. For the year of 1983, he was predicting a loss in excess of $50,000.

The beer was not all that had turned sour. Shipman had become tense and angry. He had devoted his career to the brewery, but there was no prospect of the stock ever becoming valuable. Running the brewery had become a monumental struggle for him. Personally, he and McElevey did not mesh, and yet he was dependent on McElevey.

Bowker, too, was pessimistic about the brewery's prospects. Redhook's board of directors had assigned Shipman and Bowker the task of correcting the off flavor in Redhook and Blackhook, but Shipman and Bowker didn't know how to do it. They had ordered new yeast, but it was not being used in production. At the time, it was only used for the experimental pale ale that McElevey was working on. Further, McElevey had warned them that using two yeasts in the brewery was dangerous.

Shipman and Bowker, in desperation, decided to seek the counsel of Joseph Owades, a brewing consultant and the inventor of light beer who had previously written Shipman to offer his services. Owades, who lectured at Fritz Maytag's All About Beer seminars, was widely considered a beer wizard. One of the few Ph. D.s in the brewing industry, Owades graduated with a doctorate in biochemistry in 1950 from the Polytechnic Institute of New York. For his doctoral thesis, he wrote a dissertation on cholesterol.

After graduation, Owades went to work for Fleischmann's Yeast in New York, where he worked as a research chemist. Several years later, Owades left Fleischmann's and went to work for Schwarz Laboratories. It was at Schwarz Laboratories, which offered consulting services to the brewing industry, that Owades learned about beer and how it was made.

After several years at Schwarz, Owades took a position as a chemist at Rheingold, then a prominent Brooklyn-based brewery.

While working at Rheingold, Owades became interested in taking the calories out of beer. As a chemist, Owades understood beer from a technical point of view. It seemed clear that there were calories in beer that existed only because the enzyme systems in barley did not break down starch completely.

For Owades, creating a beer with fewer calories was not rocket science. Owades knew that in the brewing process, the enzymes in beer broke down about 65 percent of the barely malt starch into fermentable sugars. The remaining 35 percent stayed with the beer. Owades also knew that humans have an enzyme called *amyloglucosidase* in their stomachs. This enzyme breaks down starch into usable sugars, so Owades thought that if he added the enzyme to beer, it would break down the starch completely into fermentable sugars, creating a beer with more alcohol. He could then add water to reduce the alcohol content and produce a beer with fewer calories.

In 1967, Rheingold introduced Gablinger, the light beer that Owades had developed. The beer, considered ahead of its time, was not successful. At the time, weight loss was not a national obsession. In addition, the product packaging, in Owades' opinion, looked awful, and the advertising was the world's worst. One of the Gablinger television ads featured an obese man eating a big plate of spaghetti. "He was drinking Gablinger," Owades would later say, "to save a lousy fifty calories." Owades realized that with Gablinger, Rheingold had made the mistake of trying to appeal to overweight people, instead of the general population.

Despite poor marketing, and a taste that some described as metallic, Gablinger survived for ten years, finding a substantial market among diabetic beer drinkers who consumed it because it contained almost no carbohydrates. In the late '60s, Owades, under the direction of his boss, gave the process of making light beer to a little brewery in Chicago called Meister Brau, which subsequently went bankrupt.

It was distressing to Owades that the beer-drinking public had no idea what to make of a health-conscious beer. The brewing industry laughed at the idea of light beer. It was considered a fad, like the hula hoop.

In 1970, however, the landscape of the brewing industry drastically changed when Phillip Morris, looking to diversify, purchased Miller Brewing Company. After the acquisition of Miller, Phillip Morris marketing executives scoured the brewing industry to see what was new and found Meister Brau Lite, a promising product owned by a bankrupt brewery. Miller Brewing Company, under the direction of Phillip Morris, subsequently purchased the rights to the Meister Brau Lite name.

The brewers at Miller refined the process for making light beer, while the marketing executives, along with Miller's advertising agency, McCann Erickson, researched the market, repackaged the product, and dreamed up one of the most successful advertising campaigns in the history of beer advertising. Instead of appealing to people who were overwieght, Miller appealed to people who were worried about being overweight. Its now-famous slogans, "Everything you've always wanted in a beer and less" and "Less filling—tastes great," would soon become part of the American lexicon.

As spokesmen for the fledgling product, Miller used former athletes in their early forties, since athletes who were playing under contract were not allowed to advertise beer. In July 1973, retired New York Jet football player Matt Snell became the first of many athletes to sing the virtues of Lite Beer from Miller.

Owades, who had never patented the light beer process he developed, left Rheingold and went to work for Anheuser-Busch in St. Louis. After a two-year stint researching the effects of beechwood chips on Budweiser, Owades accepted an offer to work for the Carling Brewing Company in Boston, Massachusetts. While Lite Beer from Miller soared to tremendous levels of success, Owades labored in relative obscurity at Carling, once again blazing a new trail in the brewing industry with a beer called Tuborg.

Tuborg, based on the Danish beer by the same name and the precursor to Miller's more successful Lowenbrau, struggled in America for two reasons. Since it wasn't an import, Carling couldn't command import prices, and at the same time, they were paying royalties to the Danes for the right to use their name and recipe. After four years at Carling, Owades left to start his own consulting business.

Owades arrived at the Redhook Brewery in December 1983. He was an exacting man who exuded a quiet confidence, and with his wire-frame glasses, trim mustache, and suit and tie, he seemed a better fit for the corporate board room or a college deanship than the musty confines of a brewery. After taking a quick tour of the brewery, Owades, Shipman, and Bowker retired to the Redhook tasting room to sample the beers.

"What is this?" Owades asked after taking a taste of Redhook.

"This is our marvelous Belgian-style beer," Shipman told him.

"Who drinks it?" Owades asked. "Is it a particular ethnic group, or is it somebody with a genetic taste defect who can't taste the problem?"

"Everybody in Seattle drinks it," Shipman replied.

"People in Seattle are not genetically different than other people," Owades said. Then he explained to Shipman and Bowker that they had a problem with their yeast, that it was strange and wild, and that it wasn't brewer's yeast. Owades asked Shipman what the yeast looked like under a microscope; Shipman said it looked like a sausage. Owades assured them he could fix their problem.

Bowker asked Owades if introducing a second yeast strain into the brewery would be dangerous. Owades explained that it was not a problem; many breweries used more than one strain of yeast. All the brewery had to do was follow normal sanitary practices to avoid cross-contamination.

After tasting the beers, Owades met privately with McElevey and talked to him about the Redhook yeast. During the course of the conversation, McElevey came to the conclusion that Owades had no appreciation for the popularity of Bavarian wheat beers and Belgian ales that contained vinyl guiacol, the phenolic compound that gave Redhook its spicy flavor.

Later in the day, Shipman negotiated a consulting deal with Owades. At the time, Redhook couldn't afford to pay Owades his normal consulting fee, so Owades agreed to a reduced fee, to be paid in quarterly installments. After Shipman and Owades had agreed on the terms, Owades wrote down a number on a piece of paper and handed it to Shipman.

"Call this number for yeast," Owades said. The number that he handed Shipman was the number for Schwarz Laboratories.

When Owades returned to his office in Sonoma, California, he examined the Redhook yeast under the microscope. It was the weirdest yeast he had ever seen; it didn't even look like normal brewer's yeast, which appeared as little brown balls under a microscope. It looked instead like sausages and all sorts of other funny shapes. Somehow, Owades concluded, the yeast had become contaminated.

For Shipman and Bowker, Owades' visit marked a turning point for the company. Now they knew that having two yeast strains did not pose a real threat to the brewery. They also knew that the brewery's problems could be solved by switching to a new yeast.

From McElevey's viewpoint, Owades' visit was strictly academic. He had already procured new yeast from Schwarz Laboratories, and his new pale ale, which used the Schwarz Laboratories #96 yeast, was ready to be served at the Redhook Christmas party at Shipman's house on December 23.

The brewery crew surprised Shipman by bringing a keg of the pale ale to the party. It was the first time Shipman had ever tasted the finished, filtered, carbonated, and kegged pale ale. For Shipman, the ale represented a complete breakthrough.

"This is going to work," he told Bowker after tasting the ale.

Bowker too, was completely impressed with the flavor.

"Let's come out with a new brand to go with this new yeast," he suggested. "We already have all these people that drink Redhook. Let's not kill that. But we also want to come out with a fresh start."

Later that night, Shipman asked McElevey if it was possible to change Blackhook to the new yeast. McElevey told him it would be no problem. For the Redhook Brewery staff, the Christmas party of 1983 was filled with promise. They had weathered some tough times, but they had made the dream of a microbrewery happen. And now they had a delicious new ale that they believed would take the market by storm. The Redhook Brewery, it seemed, was poised to turn the corner. Redhook needed to do it quickly, though, because for the year of 1983, the brewery grossed $259,594 in sales, but lost $68,772.

That winter, Shipman and Bowker worked on the packaging and marketing for the pale ale's spring introduction. Bowker, with his naming expertise, came up with the name *Ballard Bitter*. The idea was to diverge from the naming scheme followed by Redhook and Blackhook, and thus disassociate Ballard Bitter from any negative impressions created by Redhook.

Heckler designed the label for Ballard Bitter, which featured a picture of a fictitious, mustached Captain Ballard—a character based on a picture that Bowker had pilfered from an apartment he had stayed in during his college years. Bowker created the beer's slogan, *Ya Sure, Ya Betcha*, a phrase frequently used by one of the board members, Mark Torrance.

The slogan was based on an old Ballard High School cheer that celebrated the Scandinavian roots of the Ballard community. The cheer went like this: "Lutefisk, lutefisk, lefsa, lefsa, we're from Ballard High, Ya, Sure, Ya Betcha."

In the cheer, *lutefisk* refers to a textured Scandinavian delicacy of cod fish soaked in lye, while *lefsa* is Scandanavian dish of rolled potato that is served with a variety of fillings. The light-hearted, ethnic marketing campaign worked on a variety of levels: it immediately differentiated Ballard Bitter from Redhook Ale; it gave the product enormous local appeal because it was immediately recognizable with the Ballard name; and the *Ya Sure, Ya Betcha* slogan served as a Redhook battle cry that it was finally confident in the taste, quality, and consistency of its beer.

In the spring of 1984, Redhook officially introduced Ballard Bitter—their light, hoppy, British-style bitter with an alcohol content of 4 percent. Within two months, Ballard Bitter was outselling Redhook locally. The marketing strategy proved to be enormously successful, especially in Ballard. At the Ballard Firehouse, when people came into the bar and saw the Ballard Bitter tap handle, they asked the bartender, Brad Joseph, where it came from. When Joseph confirmed that it came from Ballard, they immediately ordered one— even the old-timers who wouldn't touch Redhook or Blackhook.

When Chris Barnes, the owner of Murphy's, tasted Ballard Bitter, he could tell that it was the beer that the Redhook Brewery had originally intended to brew. With Ballard Bitter, Redhook had managed to recover from the black eye they received when they introduced Redhook.

At the Virginia Inn, Demombynes and Fotheringham put Ballard Bitter on tap. Fotheringham called Ballard Bitter "women's ale" or "learner's ale." The names of Grant's Scottish Ale and Ballard Bitter appeared side by side on the blackboard at the Virginia Inn, and Fotheringham or Demombynes often explained to customers that the beer that said it was bitter—Ballard Bitter—was not bitter, but the beer that didn't say it was bitter—Grant's Scottish Ale—was, in fact, bitter.

Several months after its introduction, Ballard Bitter was outsell-ing Grant's in most Redhook accounts. There were several factors behind Ballard Bitter's phenomenal success: It was more universally appealing than Grant's; it enjoyed the benefit of local support; and it was consistently good. Ironically, as Ballard Bitter was roaring along the road to success, Grant's was suffering a nose dive in quality. Also, while Redhook was confidently expanding into new markets with its proud new ale, Grant was having problems with his distributor, Consolidated Inc., which led to quality control problems with his beer. In addition, Grant didn't have the local presence, manpower, or marketing savvy to open new Seattle accounts. Redhook, with Ballard Bitter, quickly gained the lion's share of the Seattle micro-brewery market and reclaimed the rights to its own backyard.

By the fall of 1984, Redhook was unable to meet the demand for its product. For Shipman, it was a welcome dilemma. Although he and Bowker had planned to eventually add a bottling line, they never expected it to be this soon. After all, it had taken Fritz Maytag ten years to reach the point where he was selling ten thousand barrels a year. Redhook, in only its second full year, was predicting sales of eight thousand barrels. For the year of 1984, Redhook racked up gross sales of $318,093, and showed a much smaller loss of $19,442. Even with the small loss, it was clear that the brewery was headed in the right direction, especially with the growth in sales of Ballard Bitter. Shipman, ever the optimist, turned his thoughts toward expansion.

CHAPTER TEN

YOU DON'T TASTE THE AUTOMATION

IN 1984, THE NORTHWEST BECAME A MECCA for microbrewery aficionados. Five new microbreweries opened in the Pacific Northwest, and Seattle taverns added new taps to accommodate the new brews. Beer seekers, many toting guidebooks like Vince Cottone's *Good Beer Guide*, flocked to Seattle on microbrewery pilgrimages. Beer zealots wandered from tavern to tavern, checking off the beers they sampled as if filling out a dance card.

Microbrews, only available on tap, revived the Seattle tavern scene. Suddenly taverns were filled with enthusiastic microbrewery beer drinkers, and tavern owners, eager to cash in on the bonanza, rushed to add the latest microbrewery offering.

Redhook was at the forefront of the Seattle microbrew frenzy. Bowker and Shipman primed the press with information about Redhook and its products, driving home the message that Redhook produced high-quality, handcrafted, European-style ales.

A 1984 newspaper column by Seattle *Times* wine critic John Hinterberger typified the coverage Redhook was receiving. "The breweries (Grant's and Redhook) are so small—you could fit Redhook into a three-car garage and workshop—and the intents of their brewers so fixed on quality rather than volume, that much greater expansion is unlikely—and possibly undesirable.

"But to give you an idea of the level of quality involved, what Shipman and Grant have accomplished for Northwest brewing matches what a few prize-winning wineries are doing for Northwest wine."

By 1984, Redhook was doing everything right. McElevey and his crew had improved their brewing processes, resulting in products that were consistently good. This, coupled with the constant media attention, translated directly into higher sales. In the fall of 1984, Redhook was growing at more than the industry rate of 25 percent a month. If the company entered the bottled beer market, taking on imports, Shipman reasoned, the growth rate could really skyrocket. Seattle's bottled specialty beer market was sixteen times larger by volume, and thirty times larger in dollars, than the draft beer market. If Redhook could transfer its market share in specialty draft beer to the specialty bottled market, revenues would climb to about $5 million annually.

A bottling line, always the bane of a start-up microbrewery, was often as expensive as the brewery itself. Grant, for example, spent $50,000 building his brewery, but $100,000 on his bottling line. With the strong demand for Ballard Bitter, Shipman was convinced that bottling was the way to go. He wasn't, however, ready to make a sizeable capital investment in a state-of-the-art bottling line—nor was he ready to expand the brewery to house it. Shipman decided to take a baby step into bottling by using an old pop bottling machine that McElevey had been keeping in storage.

In 1983 at a public auction, McElevey independently purchased a Cemco pop bottling line from Rainbow Pop, a local soft drink manufacturer in Seattle's south end. At a price of less than $10,000, McElevey—the bargain hunter—couldn't pass it up. He figured that if he couldn't sell the bottling line to Redhook, he'd sell it to somebody else and eventually get his money back. McElevey had originally offered the complete line to Shipman for $10,000, but

Shipman wasn't interested, so McElevey sold the filler and labeler portion of the machine to Mark Stutrud, who owned the Summit Brewery in St. Paul, Minnesota.

At the time, Stutrud didn't have room for the equipment, so he asked McElevey to hold it for him. In late 1984, Shipman, who was experiencing sticker shock at the price of new bottling equipment, told McElevey that he wanted to buy the filler component of his bottling line. McElevey explained that he had sold it to Stutrud, but that the equipment was still sitting in storage in Seattle, so Shipman called Stutrud and asked if he would be willing to rent the machine to Redhook. Stutrud agreed.

In early 1985, McElevey and his crew installed the bottling line and began running performance tests. Shipman wasn't encouraged by the results. The filler was designed for soda, rather than beer, so it was difficult to produce an acceptable level of carbonation in the bottles. It also produced unpredictable fill levels in the bottles and was labor intensive to operate and time consuming to sanitize. Each week the filling valves had to be taken apart completely so a cleaning brush could be run through the fill tubes, a dreaded job at the brewery.

Disappointed by the performance of the bottling line, Shipman made plans to purchase new, state-of-the-art bottling equipment. He also made plans to expand the brewery to accommodate the equipment. But Shipman didn't share his plans with McElevey, who heard the news for the first time at a board of directors meeting.

McElevey was incredulous that he hadn't been consulted.

"Paul," McElevey said, "we've never talked about this. I'm supposed to be in charge of the technical area of the brewery. Don't you think you should have talked to me before you made this decision?"

Bowker answered for Shipman. It wasn't necessary for Shipman to consult him on the decision, he said.

McElevey was outraged and insulted. Shipman was making technical decisions without his input, when he himself was in charge of the company's technical direction. At the next board meeting,

McElevey shocked the members of the board when he announced that he wanted to sell his stock and change the status of his relationship with Redhook.

Shipman and Bowker, fearing that McElevey would walk out on them completely, decided to consult Joe Owades to assess their options. On April 9, Shipman, Bowker, and Owades met at the Redhook Brewery to discuss the McElevey situation.

"We have a lot of tension in the brewery," Shipman told Owades. "We're afraid that Charlie is going to walk out on us."

"That wouldn't be the worst thing that could happen," Owades said.

"How would we survive?" Shipman asked.

"Let me talk with Buchanan, just casually," Owades said. Buchanan, at the time, was supervisor for the small brewing crew, which including himself, consisted of three people. "I'll ask him some questions and I'll be able to tell you if he can run the brewery without Charlie."

Owades spent the day in the brewery, examining its procedures and talking to various crew members. Several days later, after Owades had returned to Sonoma, he called Shipman and told him to send Buchanan down to his lab for several weeks. After working with Buchanan, Owades, who was convinced that Buchanan could run the brewery without McElevey, submitted a letter to Redhook's board of directors.

"I examined your brewery on April 9, 1985," Owades wrote, "and spoke with Paul Shipman, Charles McElevey, Rick Buchanan, Jim Breazale, Bob Zahler, and Gordon Bowker.

"It is my considered opinion that in the potential absence of Mr. McElevey from the brewery for any length of time, the present employees could run the brewery as it is now being run, with no danger of any cessation of activities or change in products. The men remaining—Rick, Jim, and Bob—know the plant very well, are dedicated and devoted, and are sufficiently knowledgeable to continue producing the beers you are now making."

Later in the letter, Owades wrote: "Breweries of your size do not need the services of a full-time brewmaster, and I know of none that have one."

On May 22, Shipman, McElevey, and Mark Torrance, one of the board members, met for lunch to discuss the details of McElevey's consulting arrangement. It was agreed that McElevey's full-time employment would end on June 3, 1985, and he would become a part-time consultant to Redhook. His stock ownership (904 shares, about 4 percent of the company) would be offered as a unit for $60 a share. McElevey's stock, it was later decided by the board of directors, would be sold to an individual investor outside the company.

The reality of McElevey's consulting arrangement, and this was understood by Torrance, Shipman and McElevey, was that it was a polite way of letting McElevey go. After McElevey left Redhook as a full-time employee in June, he was called upon as a consultant only sparingly the next few years, and then not at all. The reasons for Redhook severing ties with McElevey were not so much professional, as they were personal. After all, McElevey had performed magic building a brewery on a limited budget, and he'd helped save the company with Ballard Bitter. But the simple truth of the matter was that McElevey and Shipman did not get along.

With McElevey gone, Buchanan stepped into the role of brewmaster. He was empowered by his new responsibility. Buchanan was a jack-of-all-trades who could do just about anything around the brewery. He was an accomplished plumber, mechanic, and welder. He had also worked as a chef, so he had a refined sense of taste and was comfortable working with recipes and schedules. He was also well liked by the crew, but more importantly, he enjoyed a good working relationship with Shipman.

Buchanan's biggest challenge was the bottling process. Bottling at Redhook brought a whole new meaning to the concept of freshness. Keg beer was locally distributed and sold within a matter of days in local taverns, but bottles might sit on grocery store shelves for weeks.

And since Redhook was microfiltering their beer, as opposed to pasteurizing it, the sterility and filtering techniques at the brewery became critical.

Larger breweries filtered and then pasteurized their beer, applying heat to it to kill bacteria and extend the shelf life of the beer, arguably robbing the beer of its freshness. Redhook, on the other hand, went through a filtration process that involved the use of a delicate device known as a Spedoni, a wine filter purchased from Dick Ponzi of Ponzi Vineyards in Oregon.

The Spedoni was like something out of the Russian space program. It was laden with valves and dials, but it had no automation. It was actually a mesh filter, and the bacteria and yeast would get caught in the mesh. If the flow of beer through the mesh was set at the proper rate, the yeast and the bacteria would get stuck. But if the flow was too fast, the yeast and the bacteria would find their way through, creating a beer with a limited shelf life. A dial on the Spedoni indicated the pressure and flow rate, which had to be constantly monitored during filtering.

Redhook's bottling process, when finally implemented, was a throwback to the early days of the industrial revolution. Redhook hired three new employees (Shane York, Miguel Balonis, and Al Triplett) to help with the additional load. The new employees dreaded working with the antique bottling line. Each Thursday was dedicated almost exclusively to bottling. The bottling process, which was done mostly by hand, started with one person loading the bottles onto a bottle wrencher, which, according to Triplett, "broke about 50 percent of the bottles."

Next, they would fill the bottles using the rented filler, and then put the bottles into plastic milk cartons. Then they counted the number of cartons and used the number to determine how many labels they needed. Then they surrounded the bottles with fans, which were left on all night to dry the bottles.

When Redhook first started bottling, the brewers did everything they could to ensure that their products were sterile—free of yeast and bacteria—but they could never quite get it right. The bottom line was that if the product was not refrigerated, and it wasn't consumed almost immediately, it would go bad in a couple of weeks. To help their customers keep track of the freshness of their products, Redhook began to date-stamp their bottles.

Every Thursday afternoon, the receptionist, while she answered the phone, would individually date-stamp each label by hand, using a black ink pad and a date stamp—the kind with a wooden handle and revolving rubber numbers.

Each Friday, several members of the brewery crew would arrive at six A.M. for the labeling and packaging. One person would pop the plain white cardboard packaging into six-pack containers and then, using a glue gun, apply a label. Next, they put foil over the neck of the bottle using an air cylinder to crimp the foil. After the foil was applied, they used a little machine to put glue on a label. They rolled the labels, hand stamped by the receptionist, onto each bottle by hand. Finally someone would put the bottles into the six-pack containers.

Usually by about eight in the morning, while the crew was still labeling, beer buyers from grocery stores like Safeway and QFC would show up in their station wagons. Triplett said, "We would have to tell them that we only bottled so much that week, so we could only allot two cases of Ballard and a case of Blackhook."

Redhook did bottling runs of about one hundred cases, and retailed all of it. Individual consumers came into the brewery and bought the beer right off the bottling line. Redhook didn't supply case boxes, so the buyers would go to the deli next door for a box or get a discarded beer case from a big recycling area behind the deli.

With the product shelf life limited to approximately four weeks, and the need for constant refrigeration, distribution of Redhook's beer remained concentrated in King County. Twenty percent of Redhook's beer was sold within two miles of the brewery; 50 percent was sold within a five-mile radius.

Redhook's first profitable year was 1985. With the success of Ballard Bitter and the addition of the bottling line, Redhook recorded sales of $488,151 and profits of $57,876. To kick off the new year, the brewery introduced its first seasonal ale, Winterhook. Based on a recipe developed by Joe Owades, Winterhook was an Extra Special Bitter Ale that customers raved about.

By early 1986, Shipman, encouraged by the growing demand for Redhook products, traveled to West Germany to purchase a high-tech Krones bottling line. During his travels, he toured various Bavarian breweries and witnessed firsthand how technology and creative distribution enabled more than eight hundred small breweries to exist side by side in one small country.

Among the breweries he visited, Shipman made a trip to Andechs, a brewery set amidst the beauty of the Bavarian forest. For Shipman, Andechs—perhaps the most beautiful brewery in Bavaria—was a physical manifestation of his aspirations for Redhook's future. One day, he vowed, he would build a brewery in the United States to rival Andechs.

In the winter of 1986, Skip Satterwhite, a self-employed architect in his early thirties, stopped into the Redhook Brewery looking for a used keg to convert for a furnace for his workshop. Buchanan told him no old kegs were available, but Shipman, eavesdropping, popped his head up from behind a cubicle wall and told Satterwhite he might be able to find one for him.

As Shipman rummaged through the collection of kegs outside the transmission shop, he asked Satterwhite if he painted signs. Satterwhite told Shipman that he didn't; he was an architect, he said, and he'd be willing to help Redhook with any of their building needs. At the time, Shipman was having problems getting approval for the plans to expand the brewery, so he hired Satterwhite to work with Buchanan and Mason Williams, the owner of the building, to facilitate the process. For Satterwhite, it was to be the beginning of a long relationship with Redhook.

By mid-1986, the expansion of the brewery was complete, and the Krones bottling line was brought on-line to meet the growing demand for Redhook's products. Sales of Ballard Bitter were red hot, and with a new bottling line and a booming market, Redhook's sales for 1986 amounted to $702,690, with profits of $84,009.

For the holiday season, Redhook introduced an improved version of Owades' Winterhook, which once again was a runaway success. That year, Winterhook was "absolutely sublime," Bowker said, and proved to be so popular that they continued to supply it to customers until August. Later that year, Shipman and Bowker decided to replace the original Redhook, which was suffering from dwindling sales, with Winterhook.

"I'm not going to have that original Redhook yeast in this brewery any more." Shipman said. "This is the end of that yeast. I'm asking your advice on what to do. I'm telling you we're changing the yeast, but what should we do with the brand?"

Replacing Redhook represented a bit of a marketing problem. Bowker wanted to retain the Redhook name, but he didn't want people to associate this delicious new ale with the old banana beer, which was still using the original Redhook yeast.

Bowker put his head on the table for what seemed like an eternity. Then he sat up, and said. "We can't have the Redhook Ale name and change the yeast, so we have to come up with a new brand name." Then Bowker looked up at the ceiling and proclaimed, "Redhook ESB." The ESB, he explained, would stand for Extra Special Bitter, a particular style of British Ale.

Shipman replied, "OK, lets go for it." Soon thereafter, production of the original Redook Ale, and the use of its quirky yeast, was discontinued.

As Redhook's sales continued to soar with Ballard Bitter, and now Redhook ESB, it became increasingly evident that Redhook's expansion of the old transmission shop was a short-lived solution. In January 1987, Shipman told the Redhook board that they needed a new brewery. Bowker was initially resistant to the idea. "Can't we just stay in Ballard?" he asked during the board meeting.

He was nervous about the growth of the company, and he was worried about financial dilution. The specialty beer market was growing at an alarming rate, but no one knew when that growth would stop. Also, new competitors were entering the marketplace. Bowker was concerned that the market, and Redhook's share of it, would not be large enough to support a new brewery. He was also protective of Redhook's product mystique, which might be diluted by growth.

Shipman had a "build it, and they will come" philosophy toward building a new brewery. Shipman firmly believed that the growing demand for Redhook's products would support a new, and larger brewery. He also argued that Redhook had to build a new brewery to differentiate itself from competition. If Redhook stayed in Ballard, Shipman maintained, they would begin to resemble the competition. At the time, Portland Brewing Company, in Portland, Oregon, was building a brewery the size of Redhook's Ballard facility, and with Widmer Bros. Brewing, also in Portland, Shipman knew it was only a matter of time.

Eventually, Shipman convinced Bowker of the merits of expansion, and in early 1987, Shipman began to search for equipment and a new building for the brewery. To finance the endeavor, the original Redhook investors—Shipman, Bowker, and Jones—diluted their ownership to 40 percent. Shipman sold their shares in two weeks, raising $900,000 in equity capital. Shipman also secured a loan with Old National Bank in Seattle.

Shipman found a new home for the brewery in Fremont, in an eighty-two-year-old red brick building that had once housed the trolleys and crews of Seattle's Electric Railway. In more recent years, the building had been used to store garbage trucks for the city, and had, at one time, been a candidate for demolition. To equip the brewery, Shipman decided upon Anton Steinecker, a Bavarian manufacturer of brewing equipment.

The overall price tag for the new brewery was daunting: $2.1 million for the equipment, plus $1 million to renovate the car barn, and Shipman tried to trim costs wherever he could. One day in 1987, Satterwhite, who had previously conducted a study for Shipman on a brewery site, stopped into the old transmission shop to meet with

Buchanan. When Shipman saw Satterwhite, he told him they were studying another building: the Fremont Trolley Barn.

"That sounds like an interesting project," Satterwhite said.

"We've got an architect working on it," Shipman told him, "but they're so darn expensive."

"I wouldn't mind looking at it," Satterwhite said.

After talking with Shipman, Satterwhite wandered down to the Trolley Barn in Fremont and inspected the building. A few days later he met with Shipman. "If you took the current plans of the developer," he said, "and you used a different type of bracing, you could lower the cost by $60,000 in terms of the improvements."

"Prove it," Shipman told Satterwhite. "Go out and hire somebody and show me that." Satterwhite went to the engineer for the building, Jay Taylor, who worked for Swenson Engineers, and presented his idea for the bracing. Taylor agreed with Satterwhite, so Satterwhite went back to Shipman with his findings.

"Show up at the next planning meeting," Shipman told Satterwhite. Satterwhite showed up at the next meeting with Lance Mueller, the architect who was making external improvements to the adjacent Burke Building that would house the Redhook corporate offices.

Satterwhite loved working with Shipman. Both were Bucknell graduates and both were cerebral, abstract thinkers who enjoyed translating visions into reality. Satterwhite believed that Shipman truly understood people. Shipman often left him dangling in terms of his responsibility, so that he was forced to make his own decisions. In Satterwhite's opinion, Shipman had a way of filtering personalities so that he found people who could work with his minimal direction. "We should start to do the permit work on the building," Shipman would say to Satterwhite, and that would be about all the direction he would get.

At the time, Satterwhite had young twins at home and he was operating out of his house, which didn't have the outward appearance of the typical, potted-palms architectural office. But Shipman had confidence in him, so he continued to work on the plans for the Fremont Brewery. Compared to Redhook's Ballard facility, which had been constructed in an ad hoc fashion, with the wiring and pipes running as the crow flies, Satterwhite designed the Fremont building for maximum efficiency. He worked long hours with Buchanan to understand the flow of work at the brewery. His goal in designing the Fremont building was to organize the distribution of product, piping lines, and electrical work to make the brewery operate more smoothly.

Construction of the brewery suffered serious delays. At the time, there was a restriction on importing stainless steel due to a worldwide shortage, so the German brewing equipment was held up at customs in the Panama Canal for several weeks while custom officials inspected it. Finally Shipman received a notice by mail that the ship carrying the equipment had made it through the Panama Canal. Shipman was relieved. Now the project could stay on schedule. The following day, however, he received another notice that the engine room on the ship had caught on fire. The ship was being towed up the West Coast by tugboat. The delay tightened the construction schedule, resulting in incredible stress, especially for Buchanan, who'd already put in countless hours of overtime on the project.

One of the biggest debates about building the new Fremont Brewery was whether to include a pub. Bowker and Shipman debated for weeks about the merits of having a pub attached to the brewery. Both were skeptical, wondering whether people would actually come to it, but Bert Grant had a pub, and Shipman wanted one too.

When it came to retail expertise, Shipman looked to Bowker, and Bowker said to him: "Paul, the essence of retail is your location, and this (Fremont) is a really bad location. I don't know if you can justify opening the doors."

"OK, Gordon," Shipman said. "To be cautious, we'll put the switch board for the company behind the bar, so the bartender will become the company operator answering the telephone, and in the unlikely event that a customer shows up, there will hopefully be enough time between telephone calls to pour a beer."

But if a customer ever did show up, Bowker warned Shipman, they had to make sure they had a good time. The only way that they would get customers in the place, Bowker explained, was through word-of-mouth recommendations, because nobody would ever find the place on their own.

As a result of Shipman and Bowker's reservations, the pub, to be called the Trolleyman, was built so it could serve as the reception area. It was designed in the old English style, with a gas fireplace, overstuffed chairs, and a long wooden bar with ceramic Redhook tap handles. To manage the pub, Shipman hired Pam Hinckley, previously a manager of a wine shop in the Pike Place Market.

On October 6, 1988, Redhook opened the doors of the Fremont Brewery, and its adjoining Trolleyman Pub, to the public. Many who toured the building that day were awed by the high-tech stainless steel brewing equipment and the size of the of the facility. With the Fremont Brewery, Redhook became the first brewery in the Northwest to break from the microbrewery class. At the time, microbreweries were considered breweries that produced less than 10,000 to 15,000 barrels a year. Redhook, with its new facility, planned to boost its production from its 10,500 barrel capacity to 20,000 barrels immediately, and eventually to 40,000.

Seattle Weekly reporter Eric Scigliano could only shake his head in disbelief as he stared at the maze of brewing equipment. "How are you going to sell all that beer?" he asked Bowker.

Perhaps 20,000 barrels a year was a drop in the bucket for Anheuser-Busch or Miller, but it was more than the total output of all the other Washington State microbreweries combined—Hale's Ale in Colville, Bert Grant's Yakima Brewing and Malting, Hart (Pyramid Ale) in Kalama, Kemper Brewing in Poulsbo, and tiny Kufnerbrau in Monroe.

The new brewery, Shipman told reporters, was perhaps the most technologically advanced brewery in the United States. It was not just a marvel of plumbing, but of automation. A computer controlled most of the brewing process, so operators could set up everything for the first brew, take measurements at the lauter tun, and let the machinery take over for successive brews. With the new equipment, a crew of six was now able to brew two and a half times as much beer as the same crew in the old brewery.

The new brewery also featured an improved filter that would produce beer with a shelf life comparable to Coors—without taste-robbing pasteurization. And one of the most tedious tasks—scrubbing the tanks—would now be done with an automatic washer.

At the grand opening of Redhook's new high-tech brewery, Scigliano asked Shipman if Redhook was abandoning its roots as a maker of "handcrafted" beers. Shipman, of course, was ready with an answer.

"You don't taste the automation," Shipman said. "You taste the brewing."

CHAPTER ELEVEN

THEY'RE BUYNG REDHOOK IN SPOKANE

IN DECEMBER 1988, Shipman braved a snowstorm in Missoula, Montana, to hunt down Jürgen Knöller, a young Bavarian-born brewmaster who worked at the Bayern Brewery. Shipman was desperate. Buchanan, who'd accepted a position to help start up a brewery in Western Samoa, had recently resigned, and Redhook needed a brewmaster. Shipman offered the position to Al Triplett, one of Redhook's brewers, but Triplett refused it, saying he wasn't qualified and didn't want the responsibility.

In an effort to persuade Knöller to take the job, Shipman attended Bayern's company Christmas party, and amid the festivities, he pitched Knöller on the idea of coming to Seattle to work for Redhook. Knöller, however, wasn't willing to leave Montana, and he, too, refused the position.

Shipman spent the next two months searching for a brewmaster. Exasperated, he finally met again with Triplett:

"Look Al," he said. "If you don't take this brewmaster's job I'm going to fire you."

"Well, if it's a choice between being fired or taking the promotion," Triplett said, "I'll take the promotion."

Triplett, a native of Wyoming, was an ex-oil roughnecker who started working on oil rigs in the Rocky Mountains straight out of high school. In the early '80s, he worked the mammoth rigs in Libya, Africa, but eventually decided that college in the U. S. was a safer alternative to working in a country where embassy ransackings were occurring. After graduating from the University of Wyoming in 1985 with a degree in petroleum engineering, Triplett decided he'd had enough of the oil business, and set his sights on becoming a math teacher.

In the summer of 1985, Triplett traveled to Seattle to investigate the masters program in mathematics at the University of Washington. He figured he'd need a part-time job while he pursued his masters, so on a tip from friends, he met with Buchanan and Shipman at the Redhook Ballard Brewery. At the time, Buchanan was just firing up the bottling line, and Redhook needed extra help, so he hired Triplett as a production worker. Triplett's first job was hand-washing kegs, a chore that required him to arrive at Redhook at four A.M.

Working as part of a tiny brewing crew of five, Triplett eventually worked all aspects of the brewery—bottling, sanitizing, filtering, and brewing. His intelligence, quiet competence, and dedication to quality impressed Shipman, so when Buchanan became consumed with the construction of the Fremont Brewery, Shipman appointed Triplett to supervise the Ballard Brewery.

Triplett was not only a skilled brewer, he had a natural gift for improving processes that boosted quality and production. In his new role as brewmaster, Triplett streamlined Redhook's bottling line by adding an automated case filler and bottle labeler. These additions, along with a well-trained work force, bumped production from seventy bottles a minute to one hundred thirty, allowing Redhook to keep up, at least temporarily, with the growing demand for its beer.

The quality of Redhook's beer—Redhook ESB, Ballard Bitter, and Blackhook—improved dramatically under Triplett's supervision, but Triplett was only part of the equation. Triplett's costar in

Redhook's soaring product quality was the new brewery. From the first batch, Shipman, Triplett, and the crew could taste the difference between beer made in Fremont and the beer made in Ballard.

"The yeast," Shipman later recalled, "loved the new brewery." In the new, ultra-sanitary, high-tech brewing environment, the performance of the yeast improved dramatically. The yeast flocculated (linked into chains and dropped to the bottom of the tank) better, its fermentation curve was more predictable, and the beer's pH (the measure of acidity or alkalinity) level was consistently on target. The health of the yeast translated into a quantum leap in the quality of the beer.

One of the biggest taste improvements came from the automated mashing process, where crushed barely and water are mixed together and heated, at various temperatures for specific periods of time, to release two enzymes, alpha amylase and beta amylase. These enzymes, which do not share optimum temperatures, are responsible for converting starch to dextrins and sugars. (Lower temperature favors the production of maltose sugar by beta amylase, while higher temperature favors the production of dextrin by alpha amylase.) With the new automated brewhouse, the balance between these two enzymes could be precisely controlled according to the design of the beer, so that the ratio of fermentable sugars to unfermentable dextrins in the wort, crucial to the character of the beer, was the same each time. The result was a consistently delicious beer.

Shipman, Triplett, and his crew were not the only ones who could taste the difference in the beers. Customers were noticing it too. In the late '80s, Redhook became a beacon of quality in the brewing community, causing beer drinkers and critics to forget about the old banana beer. Now they were comparing Redhook with Anchor Steam and Sierra Nevada.

"My God," one customer said to Shipman after tasting the Redhook ESB made in the Fremont Brewery. "I didn't know you could make it this good."

Under Triplett's management of the Fremont Brewery, Shipman believed, Redhook went from making an acceptable beer to a great beer. And it only got better. In the past, Shipman and the brewing crew received feedback from the customers who came into the Ballard Brewery and bought beer off the bottling line. Now, with the Trolleyman Pub, the feedback was almost immediate, because it came from customers who sat at the bar. Hinckley, who bartended, answered the phone, and managed the bar, was also responsible for collecting customer reactions to the beer, which she passed along to Shipman, Triplett, and the Redhook brewers. The brewers then made small adjustments to the beer to cater to customers' tastes.

In early 1989, Redhook's sales were increasing by about 40 percent over the previous year, and their beers tasted better than ever. There was only one problem. With the new brewery, and the additional workers that came with it, their profits were disappearing. Treasurer David Mickelson approached Shipman and warned him that they needed to sell more beer than they were currently selling to break even for the year.

"Oh, yea," Shipman replied. "I guess that's true, but isn't this a great brewery."

From the start, Shipman had taken a "build it, figure it out later" approach to the Fremont Brewery. Now it was time to figure it out. "I inspired confidence in my board and my investors like a wagon master on the Oregon trail," Shipman recalled years later. "But the reality of the matter was, nobody knew where the trail was. But they sure liked the wagon master."

One place the trail seemed to be headed was Northern California, a market Shipman was reluctant to enter. For Shipman and the Redhook board of directors, entering the Northern California market was like Columbus' journey to the new world. Nobody knew what to expect. Also, Redhook was perfectly comfortable, and still growing, in the Northwest. But Sandy Monblat, a beer broker in Northern California, called Shipman on a regular basis, encouraging him to open the Northern California market.

Monblat had worked as a distributor in the wine business in Colorado during the boom years in the '80s. But when the tough times hit Colorado, people stopped drinking premium wine and Monblat moved to San Francisco to start a beer brokerage, which he modeled after Charlie Finkel's company, Merchant Du Vin. Like Finkel, Monblat represented a portfolio of beer styles, and he wanted Redhook beer in his portfolio.

In early 1989, Shipman flew to San Francisco to meet with Monblat. The two got along well, and Shipman agreed to pay him, commission only, for representing Redhook beer. After hammering out the arrangement, Monblat and Shipman called the Anheuser-Busch wholesaler in San Francisco in an attempt to convince him to carry Redhook beer, but the A-B wholesaler refused to talk to them, so they met instead with the Miller wholesaler, Tim Corrigan, one of the owners of Golden Brands.

Corrigan asked Shipman and Monblat why he should carry Redhook beer.

"Because our beer is so successful in Seattle," Shipman replied.

How successful is it, Corrigan wanted to know.

"This is how successful it is," Shipman said. "When our trucks roll down the street, mothers hold up their babies to look at the truck and say, 'that is the Redhook truck.'"

If that's how successful Redhook is, Corrigan told Shipman, then Golden Brands would carry it.

Shipman and the Redhook board decided to hedge their bets on the Northern California market. Going in, they had a choice. They could go into California and commit heavy resources—money, people, and advertising—or they could go in soft, not committing resources, and hope for the best. They decided to go in soft. They knew they could gain business in the Northwest, and they didn't want to overcommit in a market that was already owned by Anchor Steam and Sierra Nevada.

"If we can make something happen in California," Shipman advised the board, "then we're no longer a sleepy Northwest company. We've got something. If it doesn't happen in Northern California, we have a wonderful business in the Northwest and we're just going to enjoy it. But if it does happen in California, fate has dictated a bigger picture."

Monblat, for his part, had a very specific strategy for penetrating the Northern California market. His plan, which was approved by Shipman, was to pour all of his efforts on Haight Street in San Francisco. At the time, Haight Street was considered one of the centers of "hip" in San Francisco.

To execute his strategy, Monblat would get decked out in leather, hang out at the counterculture clubs in the Haight, and tell the club owners about the great beer he represented from Seattle called Redhook. Monblat, along with the two other Redhook salesmen, Mike Spano and Peter O'Reilly, had their work cut out for them. As predicted, Redhook was slow to take off in the Northern California.

Shipman had other problems besides sagging profits and a slumbering California market. In the spring of 1989, Teamsters representatives walked into Redhook's office and presented Shipman with a notice that there was going to be a union election held for Redhook's thirteen production workers.

After the Teamsters left, Shipman called Redhook's law firm, Riddell, Williams, and spoke with one of their labor lawyers, Rick Rasmussen, who told him to bring the papers down to his office. At the Ridell, Williams' offices, Shipman met with Rasmussen, and another lawyer, Herm Wacker.

To get through the ordeal, Rasmussen warned Shipman, he was going to have to place himself in his hands.

"Rick," Shipman said, "I'm in your hands."

Over the course of several meetings, Shipman, Rasmussen, and Wacker carefully analyzed the situation at Redhook. They came to the conclusion that Shipman, in concentrating on the future, had gotten too far ahead of everybody else in the company and had lost touch with the brewers and production line workers.

As the company grew, Shipman began to realize, the needs of the workers changed. With the entrepreneurial Redhook of the early and middle '80s, the workers felt like they were a part of the company. The small size of the company put demands on each worker, so everyone felt like a contributor. But now the company was bigger— thirty people—and the current workforce had a new set of social, economic, and leadership needs that Shipman had overlooked.

Many of the Redhook production workers, who were still in the Ballard facility, were performing manual labor—making boxes, filling them, and stacking them—for $5 or $6 a hour, and when the new automated Fremont Brewery opened, they felt unappreciated and feared that as the brewery expanded, they would get left in the dust. Sensing this, the Teamsters came in and offered these workers union protection and higher salaries.

Shipman was emotionally hurt by the union election proceedings. He prided himself on being liked by his employees, many of whom he had worked with for years. In his opinion, the union election was an indictment of his leadership. To keep the union out of Redhook, Shipman realized, he had to admit to himself, and the workers, that he had made a management mistake.

To rebuild his relationships with the thirteen production workers, and to regain their confidence, Shipman met individually with each of them. He talked for hours with each employee, addressing their concerns about wages, benefits, communication, how the company was organized, and how beer was made. By law, Shipman could not offer the workers more money, but he could assure them that he would make changes.

To Shipman, it was crystal clear. He did not want Redhook to be a union shop. The issue was not only about higher wages and better benefits, it was also about control of the brewery. Shipman and the Redhook board of directors worried that unionization would hamper the brewery's flexibility and sap production. In a small facility, where a brewer was called on to brew beer one day, and bottle the next, the division of labor, they believed, posed a definite problem.

Jerry Baldwin flew up from San Francisco to share his experiences with Shipman. Baldwin had been through a similar experience with

Starbucks, and he had lost the election. Baldwin told Shipman that he'd dealt with a lawyer who told him that he (Baldwin) was the problem, and they completely removed him from the process. As a result, Baldwin had no contact with the workers, he lost the election, and Starbucks was unionized.

The union election process dragged out over four months, costing Redhook $40,000 in legal fees. Ultimately, the election was held in a conference room in the Redhook Fremont Brewery. Each side elected an observer to validate the identity of those who voted and an election booth was set up.

Shipman waited nervously upstairs while the thirteen Redhook employees cast their yes or no vote for the union. Finally, Laurie Rautenburg, one of Redhook's administrators, came up and delivered the news to Shipman. Redhook had won the election: nine to four. Shipman was relieved, but physically and emotionally drained by the experience.

In the fall of 1989, Redhook moved the bottling line from the Ballard Brewery to the Fremont Brewery and closed the Ballard Brewery for good. The venerable 1950 Redhook brewhouse, originally purchased by McElevey in Germany, was now owned by Apia, a food manufacturing firm in Western Samoa that had hired Buchanan as their brewmaster.

The bright spot for Redhook in 1989 was the Trolleyman Pub. Under the direction of Pam Hinckley, the pub sold over $1,000,000 of beer in its first full year. Shipman and Bowker were astounded. From the minute the doors of the Trolleyman opened in 1988, it was flooded with customers. Hinckley booked bands for entertainment, sponsored numerous events at the pub, and ingratiated Redhook into the Fremont community. Almost overnight, she transformed the corner pub with the bad location into the center of excitement in Fremont. All while answering the phone from behind the bar.

According to Mickelson, sales from the pub not only covered the cost of the leases on both breweries, they also covered Redhook's entire payroll. What's more, the pub's performance made the difference between a profitable and unprofitable year. For 1989, Redhook sales of $2,676,108 increased from the previous year's sales of $1,680,174, but profits declined for the second straight year, from 1988's profits of $111,540 to 1989's profits of $103,990.

Shipman wasn't worried. In the last half of 1989, sales had begun to pick up, and with the new facility, Redhook's brewers were cooking up some promising new beers. At the time, the Washington State Liquor Board gave Redhook permission to brew experimental batches of beer and sell them on-premise without going through an elaborate approval process. The result was an explosion of creative new brews such as Oyster Stout, Rye Ale, and a Scotch Ale made with malted peat. Brewers whipped up a small batch of experimental beer, kegged it, put it in the Trolleyman, and waited for the customers' reactions.

In January of 1990, Shipman was extremely excited about the prospects for Redhook's experimental Scotch Ale. Grant had a Scotch Ale, which was a well-hopped English style ale, so Redhook decided to differentiate their ale by using a small percentage of peat malt, the same kind used for Scotch whiskey. In the U. S. and Germany, when the malt is kilned to arrest the germination process, natural gas or electric heat is used. But in Scotland, due to economics, peat is used to heat the kiln, and the peat taste gets infused into the malt.

Redhook's Scotch Ale used 9 percent peat malt, resulting in a peaty, smoky beer that tasted like a Scotch whiskey beer. Shipman, among others, loved it. He was so enamored with the Scotch Ale, in fact, that he decided to hold a special party to celebrate and introduce the beer. The beer, Shipman believed, was a breakthrough product, and to help retailers and consumers to understand and fully appreciate it, Shipman decided to do a component tasting at the introduction, where Scotch whiskey would be served along side Redhook's Scotch Ale.

The party was planned for the third week of January in a back room of Cutters, a restaurant at the north end of the Pike Place Market in Seattle. January is typically a miserable month in Seattle. The days are dark and cold, and it's usually raining. Occasionally, it snows. Shipman figured that by the end of January, Seattleites, hunkered in their homes, would finally be recovering from the holidays and craving human contact.

Early in January, Redhook sent out invitations to restaurant and hotel owners, billing the event as an esoteric, high-brow affair, featuring Redhook's new Scotch Ale side-by-side with Knockandoo, a single malt Scotch. To round out the white-linen table cloth tasting, Shipman asked Hinckley, who was helping plan the event, to find somebody to play an exotic instrument. He didn't necessarily care what it was. Somthing like a harp or harpsichord would do.

Hinckley, found a dulcimer player, who was playing when the crowd began rolling in on the day of a snowstorm. People in Seattle, in general, aren't big Scotch drinkers, but they love beer, especially this beer, and in short order, it was gone. A taxi was called to deliver a new keg of Scottish Ale, and in the meantime, Redhook placated its guests with shots of malt whiskey.

"Pretty soon," Shipman later recalled, "it was like a John Wayne western movie. Everybody was screaming and yipping and hollering." Then the beer arrived in the taxi, and everybody started drinking the beer again. At one point, Shipman looked over at the corner of the room. The dulcimer player was still playing away, but nobody could hear a thing. By this time, the party had spilled out of the room into the restaurant, and Dan Levine, Redhook's wholesaler, called Shipman over and told him that Redhook and K & L (his distributorship) had to put all their resources behind this fantastic Scottish Ale.

The day after the party, however, Shipman, Hinckley, and others at Redhook tasted the beer.

"You know," Shipman said, "this beer is just too damn exotic. The only people who like this beer are the people who like Scotch, which is the smallest segment of the alcoholic beverage drinking community." With that statement, Redhook's Scotch Ale died, only to be reintroduced two years later as a part of Redhook's line of experimental blue-line beers, which were introduced in bars and taverns in limited supply to gauge customer reaction. As Shipman anticipated, response to the beer was varied. People either loved it or hated it. Shipman had heard that response too many times in the early '80s with Redhook, and he wasn't going to make the same mistake twice.

By the spring of 1990, Redhook didn't need a new breakthrough product. They already had one, Redhook ESB, which was overtaking sales of Ballard Bitter. Monblat's strategy was finally paying off. Redhook ESB became *the* beer to drink in the Haight, and its popularity was spilling from Haight Street to other areas of San Francisco, and beyond.

On occasion, Shipman went down to visit Monblat in San Francisco. Each time he followed the same routine. He'd stay at the Nikko Hotel, eat sushi, then he'd get as grungy as he possibly could (which for Shipman wasn't very grungy), jump on the number seven bus, and go to the Haight to call on accounts with Monblat.

To Shipman, the clubs were the kookiest placest in the world. One club looked like a cave, with TVs, buzzing with static, along the walls, while another was filled with people with everything pierced. Some places had as many as two dozen motorcycles lined up out front. In some bars, Shipman couldn't tell if the guys were guys or the girls were girls. But he didn't care. They were drinking Redhook beer.

Monblat transformed Redhook ESB into a cult beer in San Francisco. He sold club owners not only on the taste of the beer, but on the romance of the Redhook story, complete with the struggles of the transmission shop days. One day Monblat was in one of the trendy clubs in the Haight, and he was telling the Redhook story to a young women who was bartending. During the course of the conversation, Monblat mentioned Shipman.

"Paul Shipman must be so hip," she interjected. Monblat swallowed his laughter. Shipman was forward thinking, highly creative, but hip? That was a real stretch.

As Shipman focused on opening new markets in California in early 1990, David Mickelson, then Redhook's treasurer, took singular responsibility for the details of the business—insurance, banks, human resources, and taxes. Mickelson, it seemed, took care of everything for Shipman, liberating him to focus on beer, customers, and the big picture.

Mickelson first came in contact with Shipman and Redhook in 1983. At the time, he was working as a loan officer for a branch of Barclay's bank in Seattle. When the manager of the branch, a Brit named Lou Wadley, discovered there was a brewery in town that was making English ale, he told Mickelson he didn't care what it took, he wanted him to lend them money. "Give it to them if you have to," Wadley urged, "because I want to be able to go out and have a beer every couple of weeks. This is got to be a great business, so let's go meet them."

Later Mickelson and Wadley arranged to meet Shipman, and offered him a line of credit at an incredibly low rate. Shipman couldn't quite believe it. He didn't know Wadley and Mickelson had an ulterior motive. Being Redhook's banker provided a good excuse to stop into the brewery and sample the beers. At least once a month, Wadley and Mickelson bellied up to the bar in the Redhook tasting room and stayed until they were told to go home. Mickelson, impressed with Shipman and his businesslike approach to running the brewery, left Barclay's in 1985 and went to work for Redhook as its treasurer.

In his five years at Redhook, Mickelson had seen steady growth, but nothing like what he was seeing 1990. Redhook was close to doubling it sales, and tripling its profits. Much of the additional revenue came from the Northern California market. Not even Shipman believed that Redhook could go into Sierra Nevada and Anchor Steam's territory and become a factor so quickly. But it had. By Shipman's estimates, by mid-1990, Redhook had close to 15 percent of the craft beer market in Northern California, in addition to their 40 percent share of the craft beer market in Seattle.

One day, Bowker approached Shipman in private and talked about the concept of turning the brewery in Fremont into a fortress. The idea was that they would carve out a territory and they would own it unequivocally, but they would go no further, so that if the market changed, or the economy changed, or beer drinking habits or distribution changed, they could always figure it out. They were already doing about one-third of their business by self-distribution. They were doing their own retail, they had a good lease, they had an attractive brewery, and they had manageable debt.

"Yes, I understand your position," Shipman said, "but I don't see the idea of having a powerful fortress position as being mutually exclusive with being bigger."

But Bowker saw it differently. He believed that getting bigger and building a fortress were at cross-purposes with each other.

Success created tremendous stress for Bowker and Shipman. Bowker wanted to proceed cautiously, taking time to examine all possibilities, one of which was carving out a fortress position. Shipman wanted to aggressively expand. By the summer of 1990, Redhook reached its full capacity of 40,000 barrels, and Redhook put wholesalers on the allotment system. Shipman found the situation incredibly stressful. When he visited wholesalers in Northern California with Monblat, one of the first questions they always asked was "what's your capacity." The wholesalers wanted to make sure that if demand for a product rose, the brewer would have the capacity to meet the demand. In Shipman's opinion, not being able to handle customers' orders was much more stressful than having too much capacity and not enough customers. Because Shipman prided himself on taking care of his wholesalers, and he knew that when the wholesaler couldn't supply a product, they took a lot of heat from their customers.

By late 1990, Bowker's involvement with Redhook had begun to trail off. He'd stop into the brewery to check on the beer on occasion, and he'd attend board meetings, but day-to-day management had never been his style—even with Starbucks. Bowker never kept an office at Redhook. Shipman wouldn't let him. Redhook always had a shortage of office space, because Shipman believed that office space created office workers.

One day Bowker met with Shipman at the brewery. He told Shipman that he'd come to the end of the period where he'd be giving him free advise. Bowker suggested that he put him on the payroll. Shipman refused. That wasn't part of the deal, he insisted, and he didn't want him on the payroll. "If I ask you for specific advice," Shipman said, "I'll pay you a consulting fee." Bowker agreed to the arrangement.

At the end of 1990, it was clear to Shipman that Redhook needed to expand again. For 1990, Redhook grossed sales of $4,044,371. Sales had nearly doubled from the previous year, and profits, at $389,252, more than tripled. In addition, Redhook ESB, now Redhook's flagship beer, had been named by *Cook's* magazine as one of the top four beers in America, along with Anchor Liberty Ale, Samuel Adams Boston Stock Ale, and Sierra Nevada Pale Ale. Redhook was firing on all cylinders, and Shipman believed that as its leader, he was more effective than ever.

In early 1991, Shipman introduced a bold plan to nearly double the capacity of the Fremont Brewery, from 40,000 barrels to 75,000 barrels. His $4,000,000 expansion plan called for taking over the building and land across the street from the brewery, which would house the cold storage and keg filling operations. A tunnel would be built under the street to connect the brewery to the new building. With the additional space, Redhook would add ten new fermenters and an additional brew kettle. The expansion, according to Shipman's plan, would be financed through a bank loan.

Bowker could see the writing on the wall. He knew the move across the street was the start of something bigger, a stepping stone to a larger, perhaps national brewery. Who knew where it would all end? One day Bowker approached Shipman in private and told him his concerns. Bowker believed that Redhook should temporarily stop their growth and zero in on maximizing the rate of return. He wanted to stop, at least temporarily, the cycle of risking the future of the company, growing, and risking the future again. Having Redhook stock, Bowker told Shipman, was like having a treasury bill with a 25 percent rate of return.

"But you're out there," Bowker said, "trying to decrease the rate of return, with the promise that I get to have a bigger amount of treasury bills." Bowker told Shipman he didn't want more treasury bills, he just wanted his rate of return on the treasury bill he had. When Bowker brought up his concerns at board meetings, other directors would bring up the possibility of buying out his shares. He was, after all, a minority on the board. Everybody else on the board wanted to knock out the walls and expand.

In the summer of 1991, as Redhook began its expansion of the brewery, Shipman was starting to get the sense that Redhook had the potential to become a national company. One of his biggest clues came from a visit to his mother-in-law in Spokane, a city in eastern Washington with a population of about 177,000 people. While Seattle and San Francisco were exotic islands of urban sophistication, experimental lifestyles, and cultural diversity, Spokane, in Shipman's opinion, was a true-blue slice of America. Any time Shipman and his family visited Spokane, Shipman checked on Redhook accounts, and the beer, he discovered, was actually selling there.

When Shipman returned from Spokane, he shared his discovery with the Redhook board of directors. The fact that people are buying the beer in Spokane, Shipman told them, was as impressive to him, if not more impressive, as the fact that people were buying the beer in San Francisco. It was not necessarily appropriate to bet the future of the company on what was happening in San Francisco, he warned, because San Francisco was a sophisticated and changing market. But Spokane was different. Spokane was American, and if people were buying Redhook in Spokane, that meant there was a potential for Redhook all over the United States.

CHAPTER TWELVE

NOUVEAU BAVARIAN

IN EARLY 1992, while the expansion of the Fremont Brewery was still underway, Shipman announced to his board of directors that the Fremont Brewery would reach capacity in 1994. Most of the board members believed it would happen even faster. One asked when they were going to start building another brewery. Shipman was ready with an answer. He had prepared a full business plan, a blueprint of Redhook's future.

Redhook, he told the board, was going to build a new brewery in the Northwest, preferably in King County. But they weren't going to stop there. As Shipman envisioned it, Redhook would eventually build another brewery on the East Coast, and ultimately, a string of regional breweries across the U. S.

The room buzzed with excitement. Shipman, once again, was one step ahead of them. At this point, the board had tremendous confidence in Shipman's ability to lead Redhook into the future. With sales of $5,796,551, and profits of $723,966, 1991 had been a very good year. The board had seen, firsthand, how Shipman's bold strategy to expand into Fremont had enabled Redhook to improve product quality, capture market share, and differentiate itself from the competition in the Northwest.

Shipman told the board that the new brewery would have a capacity of 250,000 barrels, a good fit for the West Coast market. It was also the same size as many of the successful breweries he'd seen in Germany. The brewery, he continued, would be modeled after the Bavarian brewery, Andechs, and it would become a tourist attraction that added to the value of the brand.

For Shipman, the new brewery was part of a master plan that met a series of converging needs. At the time, Redhook was creeping up on its ten-year anniversary, and long-time investors were beginning to wonder how, and when, they were going to see a return on their investment. With Shipman's plan, investors would get liquidity, because financing the brewery would require that Redhook eventually go public. At the same time, Redhook employees were getting older and starting families, and they were looking for permanent careers. The expansion, Shipman believed, would provide career growth and give employees a chance to buy into the company—financially and emotionally. Also, wholesalers were asking Shipman what would happen if their business took off by 50 percent next year. Could Redhook support the growing volume? With a new brewery, whole-salers would be assured an ample supply of beer for years down the road. Finally, Shipman was approaching forty years of age. It was a time of reckoning, and the memory of Opdycke's comment about the guy "who didn't go for it," along with Shipman's vow to have something big by forty, lingered in his consciousness. Shipman was proud of his accomplishments, but he wasn't willing to rest on his laurels.

As Shipman talked about his plans for the new brewery, a board member asked him how he would finance it.

"The beauty of this thing," he replied, "is that if we go through the steps to finance this thing properly, it will lead, unequivocally, to a public stock offering." It was a bold statement for a company that had only $6 million in sales. But as Shipman assured his board, there were enough signals in the marketplace to indicate that there was an opportunity for Redhook to grow into something much bigger.

Everyone in the room was immediately behind the idea. Everyone, that is, except for Bowker. According to Shipman, Bowker was reaching for the emergency brake. He wasn't pulling on it, but he was reaching for it. It was like a slow motion scene, and everybody was wincing, hoping he would refrain, because everybody else had their feet on the accelerator.

Bowker, who was already concerned that Redhook had gone too far with the Fremont expansion, asked the members of the board what made them think that Redhook was going to sell in other regions of the country? He also wanted to know what was going to happen if people looked at the company and said it was too big?. How were they going to deal with that? And what was going to happen if building the new brewery made consumers more sympathetic to smaller, more local, more charming breweries? Was that going to put Redhook in a position where they were stuck competing with Heineken, and was Redhook really equipped to do that?

They were all valid questions. But rather than thinking about the answers to the questions, Shipman and the board members were all wondering how they were going to get Bowker to vote for the new brewery. They knew they could proceed with the brewery plans without Bowker's consent, but no one wanted to. Bowker was an important part of the company, and because of his experience with Starbucks, the board members valued his judgment and counsel.

At the same time, the board didn't want Redhook to lose its momentum, or to miss out on an opportunity. They also didn't want to leave room for another competitor such as Pyramid Brewing Company, which was becoming a major player in the craft beer market in Seattle, to come along and grab a share of the market that might otherwise belong to Redhook. Although no formal agreement was reached on the new brewery during the meeting, Shipman was encouraged by the board's reaction, and several days later, he started looking for building sites in the Seattle area.

With Bowker firmly entrenched against moving hastily forward on the construction of the new brewery, board meetings became increasingly frustrating. Some suggested having a showdown or buying out Bowker's shares of the company.

Finally, to relieve the tension, and to address Bowker's issues, it was decided that Bowker, Shipman, Frank Clement, and Mark Torrance would form a committee to conduct a thorough, six-month investigation of Shipman's expansion plan. The committee would then develop its own plan to address everyone's needs. Once the plan was complete, the committee would present it to the board and everyone could vote on it. If inevitably there was a showdown or somebody parted company, at least it would be handled in a professional manner.

Bowker's intention was "to make sure that Redhook was proceeding deliberately." He sought not to cease expansion, but rather to insure that the right questions were being asked and answered before moving ahead. Shipman was, after all, proposing they build a brewery with a capacity ten times that of their current brewery. As Bowker saw it, it was critical to investigate not only the issue of size, but also of timing. Why did they need to make a decision within six months? Bowker also challenged whether they should base their method of growth on the activity of the competition. Would the market support a bigger brewery? He wondered if they needed media advertising to support increased sales. Should they diversify their product base by brewing Redhook lite, or Redhook draft, or Redhook dry? Bowker's stance was not contradictory, he simply suggested that they explore all of the options involved in Redhook's growth.

As a result of Bowker's concerns, the committee approached every aspect of the expansion plan with extreme caution. The new brewery, they assured Bowker, would be carefully financed and built, and the distribution of the beer it produced would be closely monitored to ensure product quality. In Shipman's opinion, every aspect of the business plan was so thoroughly thought out, that even if the company ran into a rough environment, the business would just keep on going.

One of Bowker's biggest concerns about rapid growth was that it would compromise the quality of Redhook's products. From time to time, he would stop into the brewery to taste the beer. We're making more beer, he would say to Shipman, is it as good? Shipman would explain what they were doing to make the beer better, how they were formulating it, how they were brewing it, and how Redhook was gaining recognition for their dedication to quality. Then Shipman would explain how they were going to brew beer in the new brewery.

Bowker was also worried about the value of the stock. I have this incredible stock, he said to Shipman, what's going to happen to it? Shipman assured him that the stock price, and the quality of the investment, would increase with the expansion. Bowker was also concerned that going public would place a set of expectations and pressures on Shipman that would stress him. He kept telling Shipman that he was concerned that the whole thing was going to be unsatisfactory.

In the fall of 1992, a meeting in Frank Clement's office at Paine Webber in downtown Seattle marked a turning point. During the meeting, Bowker, Shipman, Torrance, and Clement went over the business plan one more time. When they were done, they agreed to build a new brewery, and to go forward with plans to prepare for a public offering.

In Shipman's opinion, Bowker understood that everybody wanted the expansion to proceed in a very positive manner, and he realized that Shipman and the board members had carefully analyzed the issues. It also didn't hurt that during the six-month study, Redhook continued its steady growth.

In September, the Redhook board of directors approved the plan to build the new brewery, and Shipman continued looking for building sites. In October, a contact at Chateau Ste. Michelle called Shipman and told him the land across the street from the winery was available. The twenty-two acre tract of land had been in development for years. During the '80s, several commercial groups attempted to develop the area, but met strong resistance from the local community, which formed a group, the Hollywood Hills Association, to preserve the rural character of the valley and halt industrial warehouse development. Finally the commercial groups realized they couldn't fight it any more. A better approach, they decided, was to find a good tenant to occupy the land. Redhook seemed like a wise choice.

Shipman called Satterwhite, his architect, and they drove out to Woodinville to inspect the site. They liked what they saw, and when they returned to Seattle, Shipman called Doug Raff, Redhook's lawyer at Riddell, Williams, and told him to start negotiations to buy the land.

Shipman's instructions to Satterwhite were simple. He told him to design the maximum building that would fit on the back portion of the land. He wanted the brewery to be built in two phases. The total cost of both phases, with the equipment, he explained, should be around $20 million. The first phase should cost no more than $14 million. The style, he explained, should be *nouveau Bavarian.* "Make it look like Andechs," Shipman said, and then he gave Satterwhite a picture of the Andechs Brewery, a modern structure of stone, stained wood, and cathedral ceilings that was perched on top of a mountain in the Bavarian woods.

For Shipman, the new brewery would be the fulfillment of a vision he'd had in Germany in 1986 when he visited Andechs. Shipman was obsessed with Andechs. According to Frank Clement, Shipman talked about it all the time. "You've got to see this thing," he would tell Clement. To Clement, it was as if Shipman had gone to the mountain and seen God.

In December, Shipman scheduled a meeting with the Hollywood Hills Association to address the concerns of the community. The meeting was held at the Columbia Winery in Woodinville, a stone's throw away from the building site. During the meeting, Shipman went over some conceptual ideas and then opened up the meeting for discussion. He told the crowd that Redhook wanted to pattern the brewery after the Andechs Brewery in Bavaria.

One of the men in the group stood up. "I've been to the Andechs Brewery," he said, "and it's one of the most beautiful breweries I've ever seen. I'm all for what you guys are doing."

Another man stood up and said, "I've been to the plant in Fremont. It's very nice, and Redhook has a good relationship with their neighbors."

After the meeting, Satterwhite told Shipman he could come up with a form that might please the association. Soon after, he started building a model out of toothpicks. The model was based on a series of triangular shapes that would form the steep pitches of the roofs, just like the roofs of Andechs. When he was done, Satterwhite put the model on the ground and climbed up a stepladder to look down on it. Later, he invited Shipman to his office to do the same. Shipman was entranced.

Shipman, Triplett, and Satterwhite conducted a series of meetings with the association to discuss Redhook's building plans and hear the community's concerns. In a private meeting, they used Satterwhite's model—and the stepladder—to give them a sense of what the brewery would look like from their neighborhood. In the end, the association agreed to Redhook's proposed building plans, with one caveat. They wanted a piece of industrial equipment on the roof covered, so Satterwhite designed what would later be called *the mountain,* a peaked area on top of the building that covered heating vents.

In late December, Shipman fine-tuned his two-fold plan to raise the $14 million for the first phase of the brewery. Half the money would be secured through a traditional bank loan from U. S. Bank; the other half through equity capital. The idea was to limit the amount of equity capital, and thus the number of shares of stock issued, so that Redhook investors wouldn't suffer a dilution in the value of their stock. That had been one of Bowker's hot buttons.

In January 1993, Shipman was ready to start raising capital and he called Paul Martin at Smith Barney in San Francisco. Shipman and Martin's relationship went back to 1988, when Martin had come to Seattle to write a financial report on the Great Western Malting Company. As Martin investigated Great Western's books, he discovered that it had a lucrative line of business selling malt to microbreweries. This particular aspect of its business, high margin and expanding rapidly, piqued Martin's interest in the microbrewery industry, so he paid a visit to Shipman at the Redhook Brewery. Shipman graciously escorted him through the facility and proudly explained how well the brewery was doing. After the tour, Shipman stayed in contact with Martin, periodically sending him statements to share the news of Redhook's success.

Martin was excited about Shipman's plans for a new brewery, and he told Shipman he'd need to bring in the analysts from New York to see the brewery and review Shipman's plans. Soon after, David Gately, from Smith Barney's New York office, visited Shipman in Seattle.

Redhook was a good business with a good story behind it, Gately told Shipman, but they were going to need to dress it up a bit for Wall Street. Later, Smith Barney sent out Jim Oakes, who wrote the private placement, the booklet sent out to venture capitalists that explained the financing deal proposed by Redhook. Smith Barney sent out about thirty-five booklets. According to Frank Clement, an investment banker himself, "Usually in these types of deals, you're lucky to get anyone who's interested. And if you do, you might be looking at one or two." Redhook got responses from all but five. Smith Barney was blown away.

Based on the responses, Oakes set up appointments with several prominent Wall Street firms, J. P. Morgan, Bankers Trust, and GE Capital, among others, that were interested in meeting Shipman and learning more about Redhook and the promising craft brewing industry. The protocol was that Shipman and Oakes would make a presentation to the investment bankers, and if the bankers found Shipman compelling, they would invest in a visit to the Redhook Brewery in Seattle.

Before Oakes turned Shipman loose on Wall Street, he shared a few pieces of advice. When you talk with investors in New York,

Oakes cautioned him, it's a whole new ball game. As he explained it to Shipman, it was much the same as when Shipman told people around the country that they really didn't understand craft beer until they came into a bar in Seattle. You really don't understand raising capital, Oakes told Shipman, until you do it in Manhattan. Manhattan is the place. Shipman had spent his career selling wine and beer, but Oakes made it clear to Shipman that they weren't going to Wall Street to sell investors on Redhook. Instead they were giving investors an opportunity to try to become Redhook's partners.

Shipman dazzled Wall Street, triggering a parade of big-name East Coast investors who flew into Seattle to visit the Redhook Brewery, meet its management, go over its books, and taste its beers. Shipman started calling himself the chief executive officer (CEO) and Mickelson the chief financial officer (CFO) because that's what big companies did.

One of the things that impressed the investment bankers, Mickelson believed, was that Redhook's management genuinely loved what they were doing. "We weren't trying to be salesmen," Mickelson said later. "We were just excited. We had some great names coming to see us, and we were honored. Most people said that they were interested in our deal because of the Redhook management. They loved Paul. And he had them so excited, that they figured if he could turn *them* onto Redhook beers, he could turn anybody onto them. We knew then that we could go public."

By May, Redhook had received letters of intent from several investment bankers, including an offer from GE Capital, the standard of prominence on Wall Street. GE Capital wanted to give Redhook the entire $14 million, but Shipman refused. He and Mickelson had arranged a deal with U. S. Bank, he told the bankers from GE Capital, so that when they secured the $7 million in equity capital, U. S. bank would activate a long-term line of credit, convertible into a term loan.

In July, after a period of grueling due diligence, where accounting teams from various firms dug through Redhook's books, the formal offers began rolling in. Shipman, Mickelson, and several Redhook employees gathered around the fax machine, and started jumping up and down with joy. When the GE offer came in, everyone in the Redhook office went nuts.

By August, the financing process was complete. GE Capital became the primary investor in the deal, buying $5 million worth of Redhook stock at $7 a share. The remaining $2 million worth of stock was picked up by the Green Corp. and Fluke Capital Management. Once the $7 million in equity was secure, U. S. Bank activated the $7 million loan.

In September, Redhook held a groundbreaking ceremony for the new brewery. As designed by Satterwhite, the brewery would be 70,000 square feet, with steep, triangular roofs of corrugated green metal. It would house high-tech German brewing equipment from the Huppman Company. Capacity would be 250,000 barrels. As the Seattle press reported the news of Redhook's bold new plans, Shipman heard a familiar refrain from competitors: "It's too big," they said, but Shipman had heard it all before.

The groundbreaking ceremony for the new brewery was a big event. Opdycke and Shoup from Chateau Ste. Michelle attended. GE Capital brought an army of bankers. The bankers from Smith Barney were there, along with Redhook distributors, Redhook employees, and the Seattle media. Shipman's speech was followed by speeches from a host of city officials. Shipman even had the commissioner of the Water Works say a few words. At the conclusion of the ceremony, Jim Oakes of Smith Barney was so impressed with the ground swell of support for the new brewery, that he called Shipman aside and joked that Shipman could build a nuclear power plant on this site if he wanted to.

CHAPTER THIRTEEN

THE SHINIEST TRUCKS

IN SEPTEMBER 1993, everything was leading to Redhook's Initial Public Offering (IPO). In June, Shipman attended a growth conference in Carmel, California, sponsored by Hambrecht and Quist, an investment banking firm in San Francisco. At the conference, Shipman met Jean-Michel Valette, an investment analyst for H & Q who specialized in researching food and beverage companies. In early September, Valette visited Shipman at the Redhook Brewery. Valette knew that Redhook's Initial Public Offering loomed in the near future, and he wanted to quiz Shipman about his business. He was also schmoozing Shipman in hopes that H & Q would get a chance to underwrite a piece of Redhook's IPO.

After carefully reviewing how Redhook conducted business, Valette told Shipman that every aspect of Redhook had a unique edge to it. But how was its distribution any different from anybody else's? And how was he going to approach distribution across the United States?

Shipman explained that he was going to go from county to county and convince the Anheuser-Busch wholesaler in each area to carry Redhook. Because Anheuser-Busch had the best distributors. They had the shiniest trucks, the best computers. They always paid their bills, they had the sharpest salesmen, they called on every account, they took excellent care of their product. They were clearly the best. If he couldn't get the Anheuser-Busch distributor, Shipman continued, he'd get the Miller distributor or the Coors distributor. Shipman planned to repeat the process across the country until he'd built a national distribution system.

"What was unique about that?" Valette asked. Shipman was dumbfounded. Distribution was the only aspect of the company that he didn't have a handle on. Every other area of the business had been carefully thought out so that it was differentiated from the competition, but Redhook's distribution network, a patchwork of Anheuser-Busch, Miller, and Coors distributors, was much the same as every other craft brewery's.

Distribution was one of the biggest hurdles for small breweries such as Redhook. In the United States, distribution was set up as a three-tiered system of breweries, independent distributors, and retail operations such as grocery stores and bars. Distributors, the middle tier, warehoused beer, delivered it to retail operations, and employed salesmen to open new accounts. Large breweries such as Anheuser-Busch, Miller, and Coors solved the distribution problem by building a network of independent distributors dedicated to carrying their products. In exchange for brand loyalty, distributors received a vastly lucrative chunk of business. The problem small breweries such as Redhook faced was convincing these distributors, dedicated to a particular brewery, to carry their craft brews alongside the distributor's bread-and-butter brands. Some distributors flatly refused, as Shipman discovered when he attempted to open the Northern California market with Monblat.

Shipman often complained to Mickelson that he didn't want to grow old calling on new distributors in an attempt to convince them to carry his beer. Mickelson and Shipman often brainstormed about ways to solve the distribution problem. Inevitably, Shipman would suggest an alliance with Anheuser-Busch. If he could get Anheuser-

Busch to tell distributors that Redhook was an approved product, that it was part of the Anheuser-Busch portfolio, that would be ideal. With guaranteed access to Anheuser-Busch's network of over 700 distributors in the U. S., Shipman could build a seamless distribution network across the country. Carlsberg in Denmark had set up such a relationship with Anheuser-Busch, but no American brewery had done it. Mickelson laughed at the idea.

In mid-September, Shipman was preparing to take a vacation in France with his wife, Patty. They planned to bicycle through the Burgundy region. A few days before Shipman was scheduled to leave, Mickelson got a call from Anne Proscino, brand manager of new products for Anheuser-Busch. Proscino was conducting a study of the craft brewing business and she wanted to visit Redhook.

Shipman asked Mickelson to host Proscino while he was on vacation. He advised Mickelson to roll out the red carpet, give Proscino the grand tour, and supply her with whatever information she needed. Shipman could smell an opportunity baking. When he returned from vacation, he hoped he could go to St. Louis and talk to Anheuser-Busch about an alliance with Redhook. "Tell Anne that I'm on vacation," Shipman told Mickelson, "and ask her if she's open to a phone call from me when I get back."

Shipman couldn't believe his luck. It was almost too good to be true. When he returned from vacation, he called Proscino and told her he had some ideas on how Anheuser-Busch and Redhook could work together. He asked Proscino if he could visit Anheuser-Busch and talk about his ideas. Proscino asked Shipman who he wanted to talk to.

"I'll talk to marketing people, planning people, accountants, brewery people, salespeople. I'll tell you what," Shipman said. "I'll come down and I'll talk to anybody in the room. Anybody who shows up. You guys figure out who should be there."

Before Shipman left for St. Louis, he checked with Bowker to gauge his reaction to the possibility of an alliance with Anheuser-Busch. Bowker thought it was the right thing to do. Redhook was so tiny, he told Shipman, that he couldn't imagine trying to leave the Northwest without the help of Anheuser-Busch.

Shipman visited Anheuser-Busch on November 15. When he arrived, he discovered that it was like a city unto itself. The scale was staggering. The new product area, however, was relatively small. Shipman's meeting was attended by Anne Proscino, a couple of people from the planning department, and an upper-level Anheuser-Busch executive.

Shipman started the meeting by drawing a box on a white board. At one corner of the box he wrote "brand." At the opposite corner, he wrote "distribution." As Shipman explained it to the Anheuser-Busch executives, "you either have a strong brand or a weak brand, or you have strong distribution or weak distribution. If you have a strong brand and strong distribution, that's incredible. If you have a strong brand with weak distribution, you are an alliance candidate, which is what Redhook is," Shipman explained. "The bottom line is that Redhook needs sponsorship from Anheuser-Busch to open up it national markets."

"Do you want money?" one of the Anheuser-Busch representatives asked.

"No, we don't need money," Shipman replied. "We want an alliance. We want Anheuser-Busch to tell distributors that Redhook is an approved part of its portfolio."

After the meeting, Shipman and Proscino agreed to talk again, and a month later, Shipman returned to Anheuser-Busch. This time more people showed up, and Shipman went through his presentation again. Again, the question of money was raised.

"I don't need money," Shipman replied, "but I would like A-B to invest in Redhook so we're partners. I know we'll find a good use for the money, but it should only be a minority position." Shipman believed that if Anheuser-Busch owned a portion of Redhook, they would be more committed to making the alliance work.

What kind of minority position was Shipman thinking about, one Anheuser-Busch executive wanted to know.

"I was thinking that Anheuser-Busch should have a minority stake in Redhook—maybe about 5 percent," Shipman said. Anheuser-Busch, however, had a much bigger number in mind: 49 percent.

Shipman said, "Look, there are so many numbers in between, let's not get hung up on it."

Shipman was excited by the interaction. Anhueser-Busch was talking numbers. They were serious about the deal. With access to Anheuser-Busch's vast network of distributors, Redhook could quickly penetrate new markets, and sales would skyrocket. It was just the ticket Redhook needed to set the stage for its public stock offering.

In December, Shipman scheduled a trip to New York to talk to the investors at Smith Barney and GE Capital about his plans for Redhook's IPO. He was also anxious to share his news about the progress of the alliance talks with A-B. Shortly before Christmas, however, Proscino called and told him that she and her associates wanted to pay him a visit on January 5.

"Anne, you'll have to wait a week," Shipman said, "because I'm going back to New York. I don't want to throw off anybody's schedule. These people that I have made arrangements to see are very important people. I'm going to see the folks at GE Capital and I'm going to see the people at Smith Barney to talk about the public stock offering."

Proscino insisted that her associates wanted to visit Redhook on January 5.

"It'll have to wait a week," Shipman said. "Maybe I can come down and see you again."

Proscino told him that Pat Stokes, the president of Anheuser-Busch, was planning to come.

"Please tell Mr. Stokes," Shipman said, "that I regret that I have these scheduled meetings. I've made them. They're set up. These are my investors at GE, and my guys at Smith Barney who introduced me to GE."

August Busch (CEO of Anheuser-Busch) might be traveling with Mr. Stokes, Proscino told Shipman.

"Tell August I'll be here," Shipman answered. "We'll discuss the details later."

After hanging up the phone, Shipman called his friends at GE Capital and Smith Barney and canceled his appointments.

As January 5 neared, Shipman read up on August Busch and discovered that Busch typically arrived twenty minutes early. Shipman and Triplett, riding in a chauffeured van, arrived at the Boeing Field Airport forty-five minutes early, just as the Anheuser-Busch corporate jet was landing. A few minutes later, August Busch III, pilot of the jet, charged down the stairs. There was no mistaking who he was.

Busch was accompanied by Stokes, Proscino, Gerhard Kramer (head brewmaster), Bill McNulty (vice president for Michelob and specialty brands), and Jim Hoffmeister (brewmaster). As the entourage piled into the van, Busch excused himself from the group and ducked in the flight center to check the weather for the return trip. Shipman angsted about where to sit.

"You know, protocol says that since I'm the CEO of a corporation and this is my hometown, I should ride shotgun. But since Anheuser-Busch is a bigger corporation, I think it only fitting that Mr. Busch ride shotgun."

Stokes agreed.

Shipman and Triplett were impressed by Busch. He was authoritative, decisive, smart—and charming. As Shipman took the Anheuser-Busch executives on a tour of the Fremont Brewery, Busch introduced himself and shook hands with everyone working in the brewery—even the janitor. Busch asked Shipman probing technical questions about the brewery. It was clear that he had a complete understanding of the brewing process.

That was to be expected. After all, August Busch had worked his way up through the ranks of Anheuser-Busch. In 1957, he entered the University of Arizona in the business and public administration school. He left after two years without a degree. He began working part-time in the brewery, cleaning vats much as his father had done forty years earlier, and shoveling the pungent malt in the brewery's cavernous malthouse.

"When you finished there," he would later say, "you knew you were a man."

Busch joined the Teamsters, although he later returned his union card after some tough management battles, and in 1960, he enrolled at the Siebel Institute of Technology, where he became a certified brewmaster.

In 1962, he was appointed sales manager for Busch Bavarian, Anheuser-Busch's low-priced beer. A year later he was named vice president of marketing, and by 1974, he'd taken over the reins of Anheuser-Busch from his legendary father August Jr., otherwise known as "Gussie," the high-profile owner of the St. Louis Cardinals baseball team.

August Busch III would become arguably the most effective executive the beer industry had ever seen. He was a driven man who was obsessed with his company's success and the quality of its products. A workaholic, he thrived on round-the-clock meetings and eighty-hour work weeks. He was spurred on, some said, by his desire to match the successes of the Busches who'd preceded him. His yardstick was his father, Gussie, who—by building the new breweries and developing the distribution network—created the modern Anheuser-Busch empire. August Busch III's record was just as remarkable. As Anheuser-Busch entered the last decade of the twentieth century, it controlled 42 percent of the American Beer market. Miller, the number two brewery and once Anheuser-Busch's greatest challenger, was a distant second with 22 percent.

After touring the brewery, Shipman, Triplett, and the Anheuser-Busch entourage ate lunch at Redhook's Trolleyman Pub. During lunch, Busch explained to Shipman that Anheuser-Busch wanted in no way to influence the operations of Redhook. He also wanted to make absolutely certain that Redhook was not marketing its products toward minors.

As they munched on burritos, Busch, not a man of small talk, cut to the chase. He took a pen and a piece of paper and drew a map of the United States on it. Mark on here, he told Shipman, where you want to build breweries. Shipman took the pen and marked off a series of xs, one in the Northeast, one in the Southeast, one in the Midwest, and one in Texas.

Busch then took back the piece of paper and pen. Anheuser-Busch has distributors here, here, here, Busch told Shipman, dotting the paper with countless pen marks to indicate the locations of his distributors. It was obvious, Busch noted, that Redhook knew what it was doing. He trusted them to build good breweries. He would have his guy, Bruce Sandison, contact him next week to hammer out the deal.

Later that month, Shipman traveled back East to see his investors at GE Capital. When Shipman excitedly shared the news of the impending Anheuser-Busch\Redhook alliance with the GE executives, he was surprised by their reaction.

John Carelton, senior vice president, cautioned Shipman about the backlash of the deal. Carelton's knew that Anheuser-Busch had one of the greatest distribution channels in the world, but he was concerned that if Redhook became associated with A-B, it would diminish what people thought about Redhook.

Shipman was incredulous. "How could that be?" he asked. "We've been associated with GE. You guys have invested in our company. We made a press release about it. People in Seattle are very sensitive to big companies, particularly about GE, because of GE's association with nuclear weapons and the defense business and how huge they are. But nobody in Seattle even commented about the GE association. Forty-four percent of the beer consumed in the United States is Anheuser-Busch. What would people possibly think about us? Why would they possibly get uptight about that?"

Carelton warned that it could happen. Redhook's competitors could make a big deal out of the alliance.

"Anheuser-Busch is a great company," Shipman said, "I would love to be associated with it."

Satisfied that he had voiced his concerns, and that Shipman understood the possible ramifications of the deal, Carelton offered to help Shipman negotiate the arrangement with Anheuser-Busch.

When Shipman returned to Seattle he met with Bowker and related Carelton's concerns.

"Look, Paul," Bowker assured him, "if we're going to grow as a business, we're going to need this kind of help."

Redhook's board of directors shared Bowker's sentiment. A few members voiced concerns about how the alliance might be perceived by the craft brewing community, but the board was overwhelmingly in favor of the deal. After all, the IPO was right around the corner, and with GE Capital and Anheuser-Busch behind them, the value of their stock was going to go through the roof.

In June 1994, Shipman announced to the press that Redhook was selling 25 percent of its ownership to Anheuser-Busch. In exchange, they would get exclusive distribution with Anheuser-Busch in territories where they were expanding. Contracts with existing distributors would be honored, Redhook, Shipman stressed, would remain an independent company with control over its marketing and brewing activities. Redhook would use the money ($17.9 million) from the deal to finish building the Woodinville Brewery, and to build another brewery, tentatively slated for Portsmouth, New Hampshire.

As Shipman recalled years later, "After we did the Anheuser-Busch deal, we had to build a brewery on the East Coast." There was no argument from the Redhook board of directors. Bowker was solidly behind it. Redhook could have shipped the beer across the U. S. After all, for $20 million (the cost of the new brewery), Redhook could send beer trucks across the U. S. for years. Shipman, however, wanted a presence on the East Coast. He also wanted to shorten the distribution chain to ensure freshness in his products. As a side benefit, the new brewery provided a good excuse for going public. Because when they did go public, they'd need a good reason for why they were raising the money.

Reactions to the landmark A-B deal were mixed. When Shipman talked to his distributors around Washington, he asked them what they thought about the alliance. The typical response was, "You are the luckiest man in the world. These guys are par excellence. With them as partners, you are going to the moon." Even the Miller distributors admitted to Shipman that when Redhook went into markets on the East Coast and the Southwest, it would be well-served with Anheuser-Busch as its partner.

Shipman had engineered the largest deal in the history of the craft beer industry, but there were many people, especially Redhook zealots, who had a negative opinion of the Redhook\Anheuser-Busch alliance. Many Seattleites felt betrayed by Redhook. They thought Redhook was selling out. The word on the street, incorrect though it was, was that Anheuser-Busch was buying Redhook outright.

Redhook customers weren't the only ones who had a negative opinion. Many craft brewers viewed Redhook as a defector from the ranks. The most critical opponent of the alliance was Jim Koch, owner of the Boston Beer Company and the man behind America's top selling craft beer, Samuel Adams. Koch lashed out at Redhook and Anheuser-Busch, dubbing the alliance "Budhook."

"Jim Koch will put all his personal energy and resources behind the idea that Redhook is Budweiser," Bowker told Shipman. "Koch is going to try to kill us with this message: 'Big is bad.'"

"Yeah," Shipman said, "and we'll put all our energy behind the message that Jim Koch is a contract brewer and his beer is made by Stroh's."

Redhook tried to diminish Koch's voice with its own statements about Boston Beer Company's contract brewing. Boston Beer Company should be called Allentown Beer Company, Shipman told the press, since it was brewed by the Stroh's Brewery in Allentown, Pennsylvania. Redhook's message about craft brewing was hard to understand. Koch's "Budhook" message, however, was crystal clear, and very effective. Shipman and Bowker struggled to find an answer to Koch's assault. In the end, they decided to follow a very simple strategy: they decided to tell the truth.

Looking back on the publicity following the Anheuser-Busch deal, Shipman admitted that Redhook had erred. "It was not a mistake to associate with Anheuser-Busch," he said. "The mistake was not coming out simultaneously with a message about Redhook. Something to the effect that we were still Redhook, that we were specialty brewers, we were small, we had a history, we had these marvelous products, we were class guys, and we ran our own show. If I had it to do over again with what I know now, I would have committed powerful resources to creating a positive message about who we were and what our products were. The lesson was that when you do something big like that, you have to think about how people will react. I was so proud to be associated with Anheuser-Busch that I naively failed to look at all the possible consequences."

Ironically, after the Redhook\Anheuser-Busch deal was done, both companies received hundreds of phone calls from microbrewers across the country asking how they could set up a similar alliance. The magnitude of the deal was perhaps best symbolized by a statement made to Shipman by Sandy Monblat.

"Paul," Monblat said, "in one sales call, you have outdone what it will take me the rest of my life to achieve."

CHAPTER FOURTEEN

SURVIVAL
OF THE FITTEST

No one was surprised when in July 1995, Redhook announced its plan to go public with an initial offering of 1.9 million shares at $13 to $15 a share. Smith Barney, Piper Jaffray, and Montgomery Securities handled the underwriting of what was one the most eagerly awaited offerings in Northwest history. As Redhook's August 17 IPO date approached, the ratio of buyers to available shares climbed to twenty to one. Others claimed the ratio was even higher, at thirty-five to one. Days before the offering, Mickelson, who had changed positions to Redhook's chief operating officer, was flooded with calls. "Did you know you're my new best friend," one caller told Mickelson.

The day before Redhook went public, Shipman was in Baltimore on a sales call at T. Price Rowe. At the end of the day, he shared a limousine with Bradley Berg, Redhook's CFO, and Lisa Stein, who was handling Redhook's IPO for Smith Barney. The limousine dropped Shipman off in front of his parent's house in Wallingford, Pennsylvania. Berg and Stein continued on to New York. His mother, Shipman later recalled, was more impressed by the limousine than the fact that her son would soon have a company on the NASDAQ Stock Exchange.

The following morning, Shipman was burning with curiosity as he sat with his parents at the breakfast table. After breakfast, he convinced his parents to drive to a Smith Barney branch office in nearby Media, Pennsylvania. Shipman introduced himself to the broker at the office as the CEO of Redhook, the craft brewery from Seattle that was going public today. Word had it that Redhook was supposed to go up to $19, the broker told Shipman. Shortly after 10:30, the first trade appeared on the board. Redhook was trading at $25 a share. That's when it sunk in for Shipman; people had high expectations for his company.

Within two weeks, Redhook stock skyrocketed to $35 a share. It was added to the Northwest Fifty Index, a popular gauge of Northwest stock activity, only twelve days after going public. In the index's nine-year history, only one other stock had made the Index more quickly—Starbucks, which was added the day it went public.

Redhook's successful IPO marked a watershed in the specialty beer business, sparking a series of IPOs from other specialty breweries hoping to follow in the wake of Redhook's success. Within the same year, three other breweries went public. Two of them were the specialty beer industry's largest brewers—Boston Beer Company, producers of Samuel Adams, and Pete's Brewing Company of Palo Alto, makers of Pete's Wicked Ales. The third company, Hart Brewing Company, was the second largest specialty brewery in Washington.

Following the IPO in August and the surge of Redhook's stock to $35, the stock price slowly drifted downward and settle comfortably at $28. Redhook's shareholders were delighted. And if Redhook's new investors were smugly grinning, imagine the joy the original investors felt. Those who invested $17,500 in 1981 now had stock worth nearly $800,000, and those who sunk even more dollars into Redhook along the way, were giddy with their recent windfall.

Redhook was not the only craft brewery expanding its capacity in the '90s. After GE Capital helped finance Redhook's Woodinville Brewery, a flood of money rushed into the craft beer business.

Hundreds of small breweries all expanded simultaneously. The craft brewery boom reached its peak in 1995, particularly in the Pacific Northwest, where small brewers scrambled to increase capacity and meet the seemingly endless demand for craft beer. Mike Hale of Hale's Ales built a new 17,000-square-foot brewery in Ballard. Hart Brewing company expanded into new spaces in Seattle's Pioneer Square district. Widmer of Portland, Oregon, Pyramid Ales of Kalama, Portland Brewing Company of Portland, Oregon, Full Sail Ales of Hood River, Oregon, and the Deschutes Brewery in Bend, Oregon, all expanded capacity.

As the first generation expanded, new breweries came on-line. From the period of 1990 through 1995, the number of craft breweries in Washington rose from fifteen to sixty. In 1995, a 19,000-square-foot brewery called the Seattle Brewing Company opened near Redhook's Woodinville site. Funded by 4,300 investors, who cumulatively ponied up $2.7 million, the Seattle Brewing Company produced bottles of Aviator Ales, all with labels showing historic planes—one sporting the Boeing World War II bomber, the Flying Fortress.

In September of 1995, according to a Seattle *Times* article by Flor Angela Davila and Elizabeth Perez, there were at least eight microbreweries that were trying to raise money through limited public stock offerings. The Skagit Brewing Co. of Mount Vernon, Washington, about an hour drive north of Seattle, was offering $1 million in stock to Washington and Oregon residents, selling a minimum of fifty shares at $5 a share. For a mere $250, you could say you were part-owner in a brewery.

Brewery madness was not limited to the Northwest. In 1995, there were 745 microbreweries, brew pubs, and regional specialty brewers in the Northwest and five microbreweries were opening each week elsewhere in the country, according to the Institute for Brewing Studies. What's more, most were succeeding. For every seven microbreweries that opened, only one failed, according to Sheri Winter, the Institute's marketing director.

In the third quarter of 1995, a span which covered Redhook's Anheuser-Busch deal and their IPO, Redhook set a record for sales, which increased 68 percent to $7.39 million from the third quarter of 1994. Profits soared 35 percent to $869,000 or 12 cents a share. The August offering had netted Redhook $46 million, and through its alliance with Anheuser-Busch, Redhook was now distributing in twenty- four states, compared with six states the previous year.

The fourth quarter of 1995 was equally as good. For the first full quarter of operation since going public on August 17, Redhook reported a profit of $1.1 million, nearly tripling the $400,000 profit of the same period in the last year. The quarterly results were in line with analysts' forecasts. "Signs of strong growth are continuing at Redhook," said Scott McAdams, an analyst for Ragen MacKenzie in Seattle.

For Shipman, the five years from 1991 to 1995 were the centerpiece of his career. During that period, Redhook raised venture capital from GE Capital, the most prestigious investor in the world, entered into an alliance with Anheuser-Busch, the most prominent brewery in the world, built two breweries, went public, and started distributing beer in eighteen new states. The result was a dramatic increase in sales and profits. In 1995, Redhook's annual sales soared to nearly $15 million, with profits of approximately $3 million.

By January of 1996, Redhook was trading at $23, down from its all time high of $35, but still up 33 percent from its initial price $17. Redhook stock held its value at $23 into the summer. By that time, Redhook was the only specialty beer company that was still trading above its IPO price. By comparison, Hart, the second largest craft brewer in the region, which had opened at $19, was now down to $11.50.

Redhook hit its numbers for twelve months following the IPO. But in September 1996, although neither Shipman nor anyone else at Redhook realized it at the time, a tidal wave of beer had rolled into the market. The craft beer industry hit a wall. The historic growth rate for Redhook from 1982 to 1996 was over 25 percent a year. For the years of 1995 and 1996, the growth rate was over 40 percent. But suddenly, it evaporated. At first, Shipman wondered if the downturn was seasonal. Then he wondered if Redhook needed new products.

By October, the truth began to sink in. The industry had changed. There were too many competitors. In just ten months, the number of microbreweries had increased 33 percent from 300 to 400.

In late October, Redhook announced disappointing third quarter results, and Redhook's stock price dropped to a low of $14. Shipman attributed the lower-than-expected third quarter sales growth to price discounting in September among the state's increasingly competitive craft beer makers.

In December, Redhook's stock plunged 31 percent to $9.625 after it announced that sales on the West Coast were flat and that sales for the third quarter would be lower than expected.

"We're still very positive about Redhook and the industry in general, but we are in a period that looks like it is leading to a shakeout," Shipman told the press.

Sales of craft beers rose only 26 percent in 1996, the smallest increase in the past decade and only half of what the once-hot industry experienced in the past two years. At the same time, the number of craft brewers—including regional craft breweries, microbreweries, and brew pubs—reached an all-time high of more than 1,300 nationally. In the January 27 issue of *Forbes* magazine, an article by Caroline Waxler, entitled "Hooked on Redhook," discussed the impending shakeout:

"Microbrewers, those hip makers of specialty beers, had a run in the past two years. But the last quarter of 1996 saw a sharp decline as competition decimated margins. Picking a winner is risky still, but we think we know who'll be left after last call. Allan Hickock of Piper Jaffray thinks it will be Washington-based Redhook Ale Brewery, even though its strongest markets, Washington and California, reported an earnings decline of 22 percent amid heavy competitor promotions." As the article went on to predict: "Redhook will survive because it's 25 percent owned by Anheuser-Busch, with whom it has exclusive distribution rights. Important when crowded supermarket shelves limit microbrew's exposure."

Redhook's woes continued. In February of 1997, Redhook announced an 87 percent decline in fourth quarter profit from 1996. A few months later in April, Redhook reported a first quarter loss of $488,000, which the company attributed to craft beer industry competition and expansion costs. News of the company's loss pushed the stock to an all-time low of $8.75 a share.

In an effort to boost sales, Redhook lowered prices and offered distributors incentives. Neither worked. Suddenly the code word in the craft beer industry became *survival*. In 1997, the long awaited shakeout had begun. Grant's was bought by Stimson Lane, formerly U. S. Tobacco. Widmer sold part of its business to Anhueser-Busch. Hart's laid off employees, while small, new microbreweries such as Skagit Brewing Company in Mount Vernon and Fish Brewing Company in Olympia, struggled to make ends meet.

Shipman believed that heightened competition was only one of the causes for Redhook's struggles. He speculated that part of what excited consumers about craft beers was the sense of struggle and personal commitment of the various small brewers and entrepreneurs. And then there were all the stock offerings, and people began to appear to get rich. There were also fast-buck artists who jumped into the game. Once people found out that big breweries were involved in craft beers, and craft beers were made under contract, it wasn't charming anymore. Meanwhile people aged, new drinkers arrived on the scene, and craft beers became old hat.

In January of 1998, the bad news continued. Redhook made a surprise announcement that it was shutting down brewing operations at the Fremont Brewery and laying off ten employees. It would also relocate its corporate offices into the brewery. The cost-cutting move, Redhook said, was made in response to losses in the fourth quarter and for the full year.

The craft beer industry shakeout was like a slow-spreading cancer. Beer pundits said the industry was entering into a phase of consolidation and that lack of shelf space would likely force many small brewers into mergers or out of business altogether. But as Mike Hale, of Hale's Ales once said, "it takes a long time for a company to go out of business." (He wasn't referring to his own company, of course.) One premise of the shakeout theory was that as interest in craft beer dwindled, grocery stores would convert shelf space dedicated to craft beer to other products that would move more quickly. With more competition for less space, a process of natural selection was bound to occur. As grocery stores carried fewer slow-selling craft beers, only the strong brands would survive.

Despite the industry's woes, Shipman remained upbeat about Redhook's prospects for the future. If any brewery was poised to survive the shakeout, Shipman believed, it was Redhook. With efficient breweries, manageable debt, a solid distribution system, and high-quality products, Shipman had bolstered Redhook for tough times. He was confident Redhook could weather the storm.

CHAPTER FIFTEEN

THE QUALITY
OF MYSTIQUE

IN MARCH 1998, I met with Gordon Bowker at his home, which is much like the man himself: private and eclectic. His house is located at the bottom of a ravine, down a narrow lane in a deeply wooded area. Across the street, old-growth firs and madrona trees shade upscale homes that line the bluff overlooking Puget Sound. To the west, the Olympic Range looms in the distance. It was a rare sunny day in Seattle.

Inside, the home has a warm, airy feeling, with considerable window space. The living and dining rooms offer views of Puget Sound and the Olympics. Bowker's children, whose pictures decorate the refrigerator door in the kitchen, are at school. His wife, an artist who works at home, moves quietly between her studio and the kitchen telephone.

It was clear that Bowker's two brainchildren, Starbucks and Redhook, have brought him substantial wealth. But they have also caused him turmoil, because both companies have grown in ways that conflict with Bowker's original vision for them.

The expansion of Redhook "was probably not consistent with my own original view of the product or my projection of the beer market," he said. "I thought that a successful, small, profitable brewery was the optimum way for the company to manifest itself."

As Bowker explained, the decision to expand Redhook and eventually go public—to finance the expansion—was not easy. He was "reticent" about growth. His primary fear was that the mystique of Redhook's products would be diluted by growth and the shareholders' needs for a return on their investments.

"A business is more than simply its products," Bowker said. "One place that I use as a reference sometimes is the McIlhenney Company, which produces Tabasco sauce. They are a really single-minded, fortress company—one product. I'm sure that when they introduced green Tabasco sauce they must have argued for about four years whether they wanted to do it or not.

"You can say that the company has that position because of the product quality, but there's also a mystique built up around it. I think one of the reasons they are able to do that is that it's privately held. If it were publicly traded, could they embrace that kind of strategy satisfactorily? I don't know."

According to Bowker, the decision to expand was always a question of market size. Bowker didn't know what the ultimate size of the craft beer market was, but he thought it was better to stop expanding before, rather than after, reaching the end of the line.

"But I'm pleased to say that I think Paul did the best thing he could have done throughout this process," he said. "If we had stopped (expanding), it's not clear that we would have been better off. We might have been stuck with an unsatisfactory market share while a lot of growth and investment was being done by our competitors."

A few days later, I met with Shipman at Redhook's corporate office in Fremont. Shipman, despite the recent announcement of the closure the Fremont Brewery, was in an upbeat mood. In light of the recent closure, I was anxious to ask him about Redhook's future.

"How was Redhook going to survive the shakeout?" I asked him.

Shipman was quick with his answer.

"If you consider the number of people who want to consume unique craft beers, the way beer is distributed in the U. S., the realities of freshness and quality control, and the survival situation in the craft beer market today, the winners in today's market are going to be those breweries that have the right combination of distribution, quality control, brewery efficiency, and resources deep enough to survive the current shakeout. One of those winners will be Redhook.

"It has always blown people away," Shipman continued, "but because of the automation of our breweries, they can break even at a very low percentage of capacity—somewhere in the 25 percent range. Many of the microbreweries have to run at a much higher rate of capacity to break even because they don't have the automation."

One thing has always puzzled me about Redhook's national expansion, I explained to Shipman. In the '80s, one of biggest appeals of Redhook beer was that it was a locally produced ale. Even in the original prospectus, it stated that Seattleites preferred fresh, home-grown products over nationally distributed brands. Now the tables were turned. Redhook was the nationally distributed brand, and there were over one thousand small breweries in the U. S. If a consumer lived in a town or city with a local brewery, why would they drink Redhook over the home-grown brand?

"It's been my experience," Shipman said, "That people always prefer the finer things in life. Most craft breweries are producing beer in facilities like we had in Ballard, and you can taste the difference in quality between their beer and Redhook's beers. Just like when we first opened the Fremont Brewery, we could taste the difference between the beer made in Ballard and the beer made in Fremont. With our high-tech German brewing equipment and our experience, along with the way our beer is handled, we produce and deliver the finest craft beers in America. Sure, consumers will try the local beers, but once they try Redhook, they generally keep coming back for more. Because Redhook consistently delivers the best product at the fairest value."

Epilogue

IN AUGUST OF 1998, I met with Shipman at Redhook's relocated offices in the west wing of the idle Fremont Brewery building. Much had changed since I started writing this book in 1996. In their August 4, 1998, second quarter report, Redhook announced that it was permanently shutting down brewing operations in Fremont and it planned to sell its production assets immediately. Even with the 75,000 barrel Fremont Brewery shut down, Redhook still had plenty of excess capacity. With their Woodinville and Portsmouth Breweries combined, Redhook had a capacity to produce 500,000 barrels of beer a year, yet in 1997, they sold less than half that amount. The Portsmouth Brewery, at the time, was running at only about 20 percent of capacity.

In the second quarter of 1998, Redhook's sales were virtually unchanged from the prior year. (Redhook sold 56,400 barrels in the second quarter of 1998 compared to 56,400 for the second quarter in 1997). In light of previous quarters, where declines ranged from 2,500 to 5,200 barrels, even the status quo was considered an improvement. And finally, there was good news. With the curtailment of brewing operations in Fremont, Redhook recorded a profit for the second quarter of nearly $3 million dollars. For Redhook, it appeared as though the bleeding had stopped.

Shipman, as always, was optimistic about Redhook's prospects for the future. Redhook's Woodinville Brewery, he explained, was an incredible success, and with its revenues, Redhook could afford to support the Portsmouth Brewery until it came up to speed. Sales at the Portsmouth Brewery, he indicated, were slowly picking up.

"How long would it take for Portsmouth to become profitable?" I asked Shipman.

"Who knows," he said, "but it isn't too far off, and we'll continue to support it until it is."

Shipman wasn't worried. One day, he predicted, the Portsmouth Brewery would be a great success "We're back to where we started," Shipman said, "we're growing the company. And after what I've been through in the early days with that original Redhook yeast, I'm not sweating it. I know how this story ends."

Acknowledgments

Writing this book would have been impossible without the help of Paul Shipman, Gordon Bowker, and Charlie McElevey. These three gave me countless hours of their valuable time and provided me with valuable research materials to help me write this book. Charlie McElevey, who now operates the Pacific Rim Brewery on the outskirts of Seattle, was amazingly forthright and helpful in supplying me with information regarding the sequence of events. For that, I owe him extra thanks. After reading my first draft, he supplied me with a box full of documents—old letters, magazine articles, beer coasters, and a hunting calendar—that allowed me to correctly piece together events.

I am also grateful to John Oakes for publishing my manuscript at Four Walls Eight Windows, and to Kathryn Belden, who not only had great patience, but edited this manuscript with great skill and care.

To be thorough in my research, I naturally had to taste a lot of beer. Not only Redhook's, but also the competitors. One day I drove from Seattle to Yakima to meet Bert Grant at the Yakima Brewing and Malting Company. As I talked to Bert in his office, he kept staring at the clock. Behind him, I noticed, there was a black safe. At about 11:45, Bert reached back, opened the safe, which was a refrigerator, and pulled out one of his new experimental brews. Bert poured us both a glass. He was from the old school, he explained, and he didn't like to have someone in his office too long without having a drink with them. Doing beer research, I disovered, was a great deal of fun.

Thanks also to Thomas Dalldorf, Nelson Jay, Pam Hinckley, Marianne Van de Vrede, and Brooke Brannon. I would also like to thank those who agreed to be interviewed for this book.

Patty Shipman, Wally Opdycke, Bill Stuht, William Kouldukis, Charles Finkel, Will Hamill, Jerry Baldwin, Jerry Jones, Jim Foster,

Terry Heckler, David Brewster, Frank Smith, Doug Raff, Mason Williams, Mick Schreck, Ed Leimbacher, Chris Barnes, Regnor Reinholdtsen, Matt Hilton, Mick McHugh, Bert Grant, Eric Scigliano, Robert Julien, Vince Cottone, Patrice Demombynes, Jim Fotheringham, Paul Bulson, Chris Barnes, Brad Joseph, Michael Jackson, Mike Hale, Bill Frank, Gene Danielson, Rick Buchanan, Joseph Owades, Mark Stutrud, Mark Torrance, Al Triplett, Skip Satterwhite, David Mickelson, Frank Clement, Larry Bausch, Tom Horton, and Gloria Horton.

I also benefited from the published work of journalists: Gary Sharpe, Eric Scigliano, John Marshall, Pamela S. Leven, Michael Jackson, John Hinterberger, Caroline Waxler, Flor Angela Davila, and Elizabeth Perez.

Selected Bibliography

As guideposts for writing this book, I relied on the following sources:

Grun, Bernard, *Timetables of History*, New York: Simon & Schuster/ Touchstone, 1991

Hernon, Peter and Ganey, Terry, *Under the Influence*, New York: Simon & Schuster, 1991

Irvine, Ronald with Clore, Walter, *The Wine Project*, Vashon, Washington: Sketch Publications, 1997

Jackson, Michael, *Beer Companion*, Philadelphia: Running Press, 1988

Jackson, Michael, *The New World Guide to Beer*, Philadelphia: Running Press, 1988

Mosher, Randy, *The Brewer's Companion*, Seattle: Trademark Alephenalia Publications, 1995

Papazian, Charlie, *The New Complete Joy of Home Brewing*, New York: Avon Books, 1991

Schultz, Howard and Jones Yang, Dori, *Pour Your Heart Into It*, New York: Hyperion, 1997

Smith, Gregg, *Beer*, New York: Avon Books, 1995

Van Munching, Phillip, *Beer Blast*, New York: Times Business, 1997

Index

Page numbers in *italic* refer to photographs.